Sherrill Stevens provides a new work on the Gospel of Luke that reflects the soundness of a true scholar but the ability to put the faith of our fathers in the language of our children. He has given a worthy overview of Luke but has avoided merely repeating traditional interpretations or summaries without raising questions for thoughts. Sherrill's writings reflect his own insightful nature to place himself within the context of the New Testament times and draw best conclusions and personal convictions about the dates and times of the writings of Luke and Acts.

Having served has an editor of Sherrill's writings in the past, I now have the perspective of enjoying his growth and maturity in helping all of us grasp and understand God's inspired Word in the Gospel of Luke. He raises and answers questions when he has answers, but he is not dogmatic about conclusions for which we can't be sure or conclusions that could be different from traditional interpretations. That makes his exposition of Luke refreshing and thought-provoking.

It is one thing to be a scholar and a good writer, but it may be another thing to live with character and integrity to give strength to the writing itself. It is a joy to sense the depth of scholarship Sherrill has and to know that it blends with the integrity of his Christian life. Sherrill challenges us to know more of Christ and to live more like Christ lived and like his Spirit inspires followers who want to be true disciples.

Johnnie C. Godwin
Author/Editor/Publisher/Pastor/Commentator
Former president, B & H Publishing Group

With patient scholarship, penetrating biblical insight, and out of a lifetime of friendship with the ancient text, Sherrill Stevens launches us on a journey of discovery with Luke and his contemporaries, nudging us to re-examine and reimagine much of what we think we know. His writing is clear, concise, and compelling. We happily stand in his debt.

Timothy K. Norman
Former pastor and denominational executive
Richmond, Va.

Sherrill Stevens' *Study Companion on the Gospel of Luke* is a scholarly, yet simple retelling of the story of Jesus, coupled with personal thoughts, interpretations, and insights. It is an excellent companion source to use as one seeks to gain a greater understanding of the life and teachings of Jesus. Dr. Stevens' personal insights challenge the reader to look deeper into the traditional interpretation and application of the Scripture.

J. Michael Simmons
Former Pastor

A Study Companion on the Gospel of Luke is aptly named. Read the biblical text then a commentary and add this challenging study to it, and you have a perfect companion for intellectual stimulation and learning. This work is not Sunday School material. It seeks to look closely at issues that are frequently smoothed over in some Bible studies, and as a result, it will challenge traditional thinking. But it is always fair game for further interpretation by the author's admission. Sherrill Stevens is honest with himself and with his readers. His kind and creative writing style will inspire you, confront some of your views, and help you learn.

Fred R. Skaggs
Co-pastor, Bruington (Va.) Baptist Church

After decades of regular study and meditation of scripture and biblical scholarship, Sherrill Stevens offers this reflective companion to read side by side with an open Gospel of Luke. The book is a tremendous gift to an expert or to an entry-level reader because it includes Sherrill's own thoughtful conclusions about Jesus' life and modeling of godliness for compassionate followers. I listened as I read, and I could hear this fruit-bearing author's wise voice gently encouraging me to embrace some fresh ideas.

Laura Mae Johnson
Chair of Commission on Ministry
North Carolina Christian Church (Disciples of Christ)

Perhaps you will agree completely with every word contained in this book, perhaps not. As someone who reads the scriptures, however, you will become a better student/follower of Jesus through Sherrill Stevens' reflections on the Gospel of Luke. Stevens speaks from vast experience as a teacher, preacher, and pastor. Ultimately, he speaks for himself—having a long life as a student/follower of Jesus of Nazareth. Like old friends reminiscing over the good things of life, *A Study Companion on the Gospel of Luke* recounts for us the good news of Jesus. From a life of experience with the scriptures, Dr. Stevens comes alongside us as a reader with words of wisdom. The insight of this conversation partner will at once inform, inspire, and—if you allow the Spirit to accomplish its task—transform you.

John Norman Jr.
Pastor, First Baptist Church
Four Oaks, North Carolina

A Study Companion on the Gospel of Luke

EXPOSITION, INTERPRETATION, AND COMMENTARY

Sherrill Gardner Stevens

© 2019
Published in the United States by Nurturing Faith Inc., Macon GA,
www.nurturingfaith.net.

Library of Congress Cataloging-in-Publication Data is available.

ISBN: 978-1-63528-066-1

Contents

Dedication

To Marguerite,
Queen of my heart
Soulmate of my life
Muse of my dreams

Introduction and
Pre-Nativity Events

(1:1-4)

Luke is the third of four Gospels in our Christian New Testament, and one of the Synoptic Gospels. Matthew, Mark, and Luke take a similar approach to telling the events in the life and teachings of Jesus, whereas John is quite different in approach and content. The Third Gospel bears the name of Luke, though the name of the author is not identified in the text. From earliest Christian tradition it has been agreed that the author of Luke and Acts was an associate of Paul on his second and third missionary journeys. So, what do we know about the author of Luke-Acts?

- He first appears in the text at Troas where he joins Paul to go over into Macedonia (Acts 16:10).
- He identifies himself as one of the "we/us" references in Acts (20:5-16, 21:1-18, 27:1-28:16).
- He was a physician and a Gentile (Col. 4:14) and a native of the northwestern section of the Roman province of Asia (modern Turkey).
- He was one of Paul's loyal associates during Paul's Roman imprisonment (Philem. 23-24).

From these references it is clear that Luke went to Jerusalem with Paul at the end of the third journey. He is not mentioned during the two years Paul was in prison in Caesarea, but he was with Paul when Paul was sent as a prisoner from Caesarea to Rome, and he was with Paul when they arrived in Rome. This information helps when trying to establish when the Luke-Acts documents were written.

Most documentary historians place the writing of Luke-Acts after the destruction of Jerusalem approximately seventy years after Christ.[1] I am persuaded otherwise. There is strong traditional evidence that Paul and Luke, and Peter and Mark, were in Rome by the late 50s CE and that both Paul and Peter were martyred in the chaos and persecutions during the Neronian period CE 62–68. There is no evidence that they were ever associated with each other during that time. It is widely believed that Mark wrote the first gospel, using as his records information Peter furnished. Most of the Mark document is also included in the Matthew and Luke documents. The Luke-Acts documents end with Paul imprisoned in Rome (see Acts 28:30-31).

These historical traditions lead me to believe that Mark wrote while Peter was alive, that Luke had access to a copy of Mark's writing, and that Luke wrote Luke-Acts before he knew the outcome of Paul's appeal to the emperor that evidently resulted in Paul's death. This evidence indicates the Gospel of Mark and the Luke-Acts documents were written before CE 65–68. The church father Jerome in the fourth century and Adolph von Harnack, a highly regarded German historical theologian in the nineteenth century, also concluded that Luke-Acts was written before CE 65.[2]

Luke's Gospel has some distinguishing characteristics. It is the most universal of the Gospels in its perspective, including more about the ways Jesus showed concern and acceptance for Gentiles and the outcasts of the populace. Luke wrote to Theophilus that he had carefully researched his material to ensure its accuracy. It is interesting to note that Luke went to Jerusalem with Paul and left Caesarea with Paul when he was sent as a prisoner to Rome, but apparently Luke was not confined to prison himself. So, if that is correct, Luke would have had at least two years to seek out people who had been associated with Jesus, and maybe even visit Mary in Nazareth, to obtain accurate information about Jesus from eye-witness associates. Luke describes how Jesus dealt with women in ways that lifted them above the cultural norms of that time in Jewish society. These attractive features of Luke-Acts make this a favorite portion of the New Testament for many people. Let's search through it for light, truth, and inspiration.

Luke begins with his motivation and basis for writing: "having had perfect understanding of all things from the very first" (KJV); "since I have carefully investigated everything from the beginning" (NIV); "having followed all things closely for some time past" (RSV). The Greek word is *akribos*, which means "to enquire with exactness, to trace out accurately, to learn carefully."

Luke makes no claim to have been inspired or ordered by God to write the record, but deems it good to write for Theophilus so that he might have "the truth concerning the things of which you have been informed." We don't know the identity of Theophilus, his relation to Luke, or if he had asked Luke about the Christian movement. The name Theophilus comes from the Greek words *theos* (God) and *philia* (friendship love), and can be translated "loved by God," "lover of God," or "friend of God." We have no indication if Luke used "Theophilus" as a proper name or as a title of honor. Luke refers to him as "most excellent," a title used when describing Roman nobles and high officials.

We need to remember that the documents found in the Bible were "people stories" for a long time before churches generations later elevated them to the status of "sacred writings." They were the writers' convictions about God's nature and character, God's requirements of people, the meaning of natural events, the outcome of national and cultural events, and current affairs. As such, the writers' works were colored by their own non-scientific status, the superstitions and folk tales of their culture, the prevalent religious thought of their day, and the filters of their own beliefs.

I believe that behind these stories there exists some basis in a factual happening, and God's ever-present Spirit seeking to guide humankind ever upward to higher and truer understanding and acceptance of truth, goodness, and a better quality of life. Taking both the divine and the human into account, I seek to find the meaning in each story that helps me toward understanding the higher revelation Jesus made about God, about us, and about life.

NOTES

[1]The establishment of the BC/AD system for dating years and events did not develop until after AD 500. For this writing I will use the more contemporary designations BCE (Before the Common Era) instead of BC, and CE (the Common Era) instead of AD.

[2]G.H.C Macgregor, "The Acts of the Apostles (Exegesis)," *The Interpreter's Bible*, vol. 9 (Nashville: Abingdon, 1954), 349-52.

EDITOR'S NOTE

In the chapters that follow, the author's remarks are divided into three sections:

1. Exposition (study or discussion of the biblical text; appears in regular text font)
2. **Interpretation (analysis or background on the biblical text; appears in bold type)**
3. *Commentary (editorial or application of the biblical text; appears in italics)*

Nativity and Childhood Stories

(Luke 1:5–2:52)

BEFORE THE BIRTH OF JESUS

(1:5-25)

Luke begins his story by telling about the birth of a boy named John, identifying the timeline of the event by naming rulers and/or natural events of the period—as was the tradition, passed down generation to generation by memory until they were written. The events recorded here happen in the days of Herod and involve a Hebrew priest named Zechariah and his wife Elizabeth.

While the old priest is in the temple burning incense at the altar, he sees a vision informing him that Elizabeth will give birth to a son. The very idea is naturally unthinkable to him at their age, and the experience is so awesomely shocking that Zechariah is struck dumb. Sometime later Elizabeth does become pregnant.

Stories of miraculous births to old women were not unheard of, though they were not common, in ancient times. Remember, for example, the birth of Isaac to Abraham and Sarah (Genesis 16). We do not know what to make of this, for these stories come from a primitive time when people knew little about human reproduction. And, the story had been told and retold for half a century before Luke learned of it and then wrote it down. We do know, however, a background for this story with its reference that the child to be born (John) would be the hoped-for "Elijah."

The origin and development of that tradition and hope followed the kingdom period of Hebrew history—from the reign of Saul, the first king, until Jerusalem was destroyed and the Babylonian Exile began. After the Exile the Hebrews did not again have an independent nation. While they lived in subservience under the dominance of other empires (after 500 BCE), there arose a dream among the Hebrews that God would raise up a descendant of David to be a divinely anointed king (a messiah). This Son of David would be able to raise a victorious army, throw off the oppressors, and make Israel a mighty nation again.

The prophet Elijah, who was reported to have been taken to heaven without dying (2 Kgs. 2:1-12), would return ahead of the Messiah to prepare the way for him. Zechariah and Elizabeth's son John (the Baptist or Baptizer, as we know him) would become that forerunner.

MARY'S AWESOME MESSAGE
(1:26-38)

During the time Elizabeth is pregnant ("the sixth month," v. 26), Mary experiences an event called "the Visitation" or "the Annunciation." As the story goes, an angel appears to Mary and tells her she will bear a son who is to be named Jesus ("the Lord is salvation"). He will be called "the Son of the Most High God" and will be given "the throne of his father David." These descriptions fit exactly the tradition of messianic hope that have developed among the Hebrews for the past five hundred years.

Mary protests that this is not possible: "seeing I know not a man" (KJV), "since I am a virgin" (NIV), "since I have no husband" (RSV). The KJV uses a literal translation of "to know" in a traditional way to refer to having sexual intercourse, as in "Now Adam knew Eve his wife and she conceived and bore Cain" (Gen. 4:1). The "visitor" tells Mary the Holy Spirit will cause her pregnancy and that her child will be the Son of God. Mary's aged kinswoman Elizabeth is also pregnant, for "with God nothing will be impossible."

MARY'S RESPONSE TO THE ANNUNCIATION
(1:39-56)

After the visitation by the angel, Mary travels from Nazareth in Galilee to visit Elizabeth in the hill country of Judah (Judea), evidently near Jerusalem. The two women share their reactions to their unexpected pregnancies. Elizabeth understands Mary's fetal condition to be a "sign," and the tradition develops that the "sign" is the hoped-for Messiah.

In response, Mary affirms with acceptance the role that has been identified for her. She describes herself as being a willingly faithful "handmaid of the Lord," and voices the beautiful "Magnificat" of praise that sings of her joy at being chosen by God and that proclaims her people's national messianic hope.

Mary remains with Elizabeth for "about three months" (v. 56) before returning home shortly before Elizabeth gives birth to John.

Note the phrase, ". . . his mercy is on those who fear him . . ." (v. 50). In this context the "fear of the Lord" does not mean to be so afraid of God as to experience terror. The things Mary describes as being done by God are all about beneficent blessings for his people. Hence a more appropriate experience and translation would be to have such awe at the majesty and blessings of God that we are bowed down with reverence and gratitude before him.

JOHN'S BIRTH
(1:57-80)

According to Hebrew custom, a week after a boy's birth he is to be circumcised and named. When Elizabeth and Zechariah's friends and kindred gather for this ritual and celebration, they expect the boy to be named after his father. Elizabeth replies that he will be named John. The others are astounded, thinking she must be wrong, and make signs to Zechariah to obtain his answer.

Zechariah is still speechless, however, so he asks for a tablet and writes "His name is John." His speechless time then ends, and he sings a beautiful song ("The Benedictus") about the blessings from God and the role John will fulfill—the proclamations that describe expectations in the Jewish messianic hope. The summary statement (v. 80) declares that all is now in order for the birth of Jesus.

THE BIRTH OF JESUS
(2:1-20)

Luke 2 begins with the familiar story about a Roman census taken to provide a basis for the regional assessment of taxes. The identification of Quirinius (Cyrenius) as governor of Syria and the taking of a census seem appropriate to the time, for when the Roman army defeated the Maccabeans (63 BCE), the empire absorbed Palestine as a vassal state into the Roman province of Syria.

Mary and Joseph journey to Bethlehem for the census, a story unique to Luke, as are the accounts of the birth of John, the annunciation to Mary, the trip from Nazareth (Mary's hometown) to Bethlehem, the birth of the child in a stable, the announcement by angels to shepherds, and the visitation by shepherds to the stable. Luke's nativity record reflects the Lukan tradition of emphasis on ordinary people.

Matthew makes no mention of Nazareth until after the birth of Jesus in Bethlehem, the flight to Egypt to escape the massacre of Bethlehem infants by Herod, and the return from Egypt after Herod dies. Learning that Herod's son Archelaus has become ruler over Judea, Joseph, Mary's betrothed, fears to go there and instead takes up residence in Nazareth. I know of no evidence that resolves the question of the couple's original place of residence.

The stories about the visit of the magi, the slaughter of the innocents, and the flight to Egypt are "M" (Matthew) material and do not appear anywhere else. Matthew's account assumes that Mary and Joseph remain citizens of Bethlehem until after the flight to Egypt and relocation to Nazareth. Matthew's record also has the magi visiting the family in "the house," not the stable, followed by the flight to Egypt to escape Herod's slaughter of infants up to two years old, indicating a possible lengthy period, and after the return from

Egypt going to make their home in Nazareth, which has not been indicated by Matthew as their home before Jesus' birth.

The best evidence seems to be that the M tradition developed in Jerusalem where stories about Herod would abound. On the other hand, while Paul was in prison in Caesarea, Luke may have had the freedom to visit Mary in nearby Nazareth and learn from her the nativity stories he included.

When the records in the Synoptic Gospels are compared, the following structural details are found that can help as we study the traditions included and try to understand the background of those different traditions.

- Mark was evidently written first because almost all of Mark is included in Matthew and Luke, much of it word for word.
- Matthew and Luke contain material common to both but not in Mark. This material is identified as "Q" (from *Quelle* = source).
- Matthew includes material not found in Mark or Luke, and that is identified as "M."
- Luke has material absent from Matthew or Mark, and that is identified as "L."

POST-NATIVITY STORIES
(2:21-39)

Luke 2 continues with mention of the circumcision of Jesus after eight days, the purification rituals for Mary after forty days (as required in Lev. 12:2-8), and the adorations of Simeon and Anna.

An elderly resident of Jerusalem, Simeon comes to the temple anticipating "the consolation of Israel" (v. 25, consolation = *paraklesin*, or "God coming near to help"). He is convinced he will see the Messiah before his death. Upon taking the child into his arms, Simeon sings about what the birth of the Lord's Christ will mean: "salvation to all peoples" and "light of revelation to the Gentiles."

Simeon's blessing on the Christ Child harks back to God's covenant with Abraham that he and his descendants would be a channel through which "all the families of the earth shall be blessed" (Gen. 12:3). The history of the centuries between Abraham and Jesus, however, reflects that the Jews divide humanity into Jews and Gentiles and claim that God's promises are exclusive to Jews, while disregarding any assigned mission by God to bring light to the Gentiles. The birth of Jesus means that "all people" and "whosoever will" are included in God's will.

Anna, a widow who does not leave the temple—that is, the temple area, for she is restricted to the "court of the women"—also speaks of the child to "all who were looking for the redemption of Jerusalem" (part of the messianic hope that the Messiah will raise a mighty army, cast out the Romans, and restore Jerusalem again to prominence and prosperity).

Both Simeon and Anna believe they have special insight (revelation) about Jesus being the hoped-for Messiah. After the blessings by Simeon and Anna in the temple, Mary and Joseph and their child complete the ritual requirements of circumcision, naming, and purification before returning home to Nazareth.

THE PASSOVER TRIP TO JERUSALEM
(2:41-52)

Luke skips from the infancy narrative to Jesus' pilgrimage to Jerusalem with his family at age twelve, an account exclusive to Luke and the only childhood story about Jesus recorded in the New Testament. The pilgrims travel in a group, for fellowship and protection we assume, so on their return travel the boy's parents do not miss him through the first day. At day's end they discover he is not with them, so they travel back to Jerusalem and "after three days" they find him in the temple among the rabbis. The story records his exceptional interest and insight among the religious leaders, and also affirms the normalcy of his childhood as part of the carpenter's family.

Transition into Ministry

(3:1–4:13)

THE MINISTRY OF JOHN

(3:1-20)

John ministers in the wilderness, preaching and baptizing. Washings have long been practiced among Jews as a cleansing ritual, with immersion as a form intended to wash away Gentile uncleanness from non-Jews seeking to become proselytes. John's baptism reflects a major refocus on the meaning of immersion. His preaching of repentance is the basis for his practice of baptizing "children of Abraham." Instead of ritual cleansing, John's baptism focuses on a witness of conversion to a changed life (see v. 8: "bear fruits that befit repentance"). He heralds the hope the Messiah will bring (v. 16) and preaches "good news to the people" (v. 18).

THE BAPTISM OF JESUS

(3:21-22)

Luke merely records that Jesus' baptism happens and Jesus is affirmed by the dove and the voice as "my beloved Son." (Matt. 3:13-17 records more interpretation of his baptism's meaning.) We have no genuine understanding of the purpose of this event, as Jesus had no need for ritual cleansing nor for immersion. And he had no reason to witness a repentant conversion of his life as John preached, and as the Christian understanding of repentance, forgiveness, new birth, and new spiritual life later developed. Perhaps Jesus was simply expressing his oneness with humanity, which needs transformation in life and reconciliation with God.

THE HEBREW GENEALOGY OF JESUS

(3:23-38)

Except for listing numerous fathers and sons dating back to Adam, using different names for the same person, and spelling some names differently, Luke's genealogy follows much of Matthew's. They both affirm the human lineage of Jesus, including "anchor" people such as:

• Abraham, the patriarchal giant and origin of the "covenant people" tradition in Hebrew life
• David, the king who reigned during the golden age of the kingdom era of Israelite history

• Zerubbabel, a key leader among the remnant of Babylonian exiles who returned to Judea to restore and continue the Jewish heritage of what has been Hebrew/Israelite/Jewish faith

---

We do not need to reconcile the ancestry accounts of Matthew and Luke; seeking to understand the different traditions behind these records and determining what is helpful are sufficient. Although Luke's information comes from a tradition that developed in the Greek/Gentile world and Matthew's record comes from a Jewish/Palestine background,[1] both affirm a witness that God was faithfully at work enlightening and guiding a foundation of faith that led to what Paul called "the fullness of time" (Gal. 4:4) when God would make his personal self-revelation through incarnation.

The genealogies tell us the Hebrew/Israelite/Jewish people were a noble people, deeply devoted to their tribal/ethnic/religious heritage, and faithfully committed to the God of their ancient covenant. Luke's insistence on tracing the lineage all the way back to Adam affirms his focus on the inclusion of all humankind in the scope of God's people—the awesomely wonderful declaration that "God so loved the world . . ."

THE TEMPTATION RECORD

(4:1-13)

I am persuaded that Jesus' temptation experiences are not about Jesus being tempted to do evil himself, but about Jesus having to make choices about how he will accomplish the revealing and reconciling work with humanity for which he has become incarnate. The temptations reflect three possible ways he can approach his work and seek human reconciliation with God.[2]

Before examining the tests, consider these cautions and explanations:

• Don't get tangled up in the matter of whether Jesus could survive forty days without eating. Numbers in the Bible are often approximations instead of definite numbers. "Forty days" means "quite a while."
• Don't be troubled by the reference to Jesus being tempted by the devil; it is simply the understanding of people in his day. In *The Message* paraphrase of James 1:13-15, Eugene Peterson writes: "The temptation to give in to evil comes from us and only us. We have no one to blame but the leering, seducing flare-up of our own lust."[3]
• The expression, "If you are the Son of God," should be translated "Since you are the Son of God," why don't you . . .? The Greek term has a primary usage to mean that the "condition" is assumed to be factually real rather than a conditional situation.[4]

The first test, "Command this stone to become bread," challenges Jesus' divine power: Because he is hungry, there is no reason not to use his ability to provide for himself something he needs. The "testing" feature of this experience seems to regard the choice Jesus is making about how he will perform his reconciling mission among people.

Stories from the Gospels reflect clearly that "if you will feed them, they will come." Two major stories tell about miraculous feedings, about how overwhelmed and impressed the crowds are, and how anxious they are to buy into following one who can do that for them. Jesus clearly states, "Not what goes into the mouth defiles a man, but what comes out of the mouth" (Matt. 15:11) and "For out of the heart come evil thoughts" (Matt. 15:19).

Jesus knows that feeding hungry people is important, but doing so will not necessarily change their lives and their relationship with God. So, as he wrestles with a decision about how to win humanity to faith and reconciliation, he chooses not to follow the course of providing physical needs and satisfying people's wishes as the way to transform their lives and reconcile them to harmony with God.

The second test (third in Matthew), "I will give you authority and glory (over the kingdoms of the world) if you will worship me," focuses on how Jesus can consider using political and/or religious authority. However, even if he chooses to use this power, the question will remain: If he controls people, can he make them change their minds, their faith, and their lives?

The Jewish system of religious hierarchy with authoritarian priests, required rituals, and a complex system of Mosaic legal guides had not helped the covenant people stay faithful to God. Jesus turns away from being the best of rabbis to instead become an itinerant teacher, a friend of the masses, a supplier of needs as he meets them—living out a ministry of service, exemplifying the meaning of a life lived in harmony with God's values.

Jesus reveals God as the Heavenly Father whose heart is love, whose desire is forgiveness and reconciliation, and whose yearning is to enfold all humanity in his grace. Jesus deals with all people as persons who are able to hear the "good news" of love, believe in the proffered love and grace of God, choose to trust his revelation of God, and make a faith commitment to a life of devotion to God.

The third test (second in Matthew), "Throw yourself down from here (from a high peak of the temple wall)," is a temptation to astound people with "wonders." Jesus knows that any spectacular event will draw a crowd, but it won't change anyone's morals or relationship to God. So, if the idea is even a test to Jesus, he rejects it as a way to reconcile people to God. He chooses to turn away from free food and wonder-working as ways to reconcile sinful humanity to God.

The Gospel stories record the reactions of people as they witness the miracles Jesus performs. Seeking miraculous physical healings and seeing Jesus do awesome "wonders" are the two most extensive recorded reasons that crowds seek out, crowd around, and are awed by Jesus. But again, Jesus knows well, and his experience proves it, that just seeing someone do impressive things will not cause people to reorder their values or change their relationship with God. In the Gospel records the crowds just bring more people to be healed or they talk about what they have seen. They are more interested in the wonders Jesus does than in what he is teaching about God and life.

...

I am convinced that one of the most divinely inspired things Paul ever wrote is the statement in 2 Corinthians 5:19 that "in Christ God was reconciling the world unto himself, not counting their trespasses against them, and entrusting to us the message of reconciliation" (i.e. the good news of the gospel). That is what the Incarnation of the Eternal Son in the person of Jesus of Nazareth is all about.

It is a basic truth that ever since the human species evolved to the height of having capacity to reason, make choices of moral and spiritual values by free will, and live life and pursue value by those choices of free will, there has been enough of arrogance in the human spirit to think "I" know better than God about what will make me happy and enable me to get my life to turn out like I want it to" (see the story of the Garden of Eden in Genesis 3). I am convinced that James 1:13-15 reveals the correct meaning of temptation, that temptation does not come from outside us from the influence of an evil demigod (Satan), but from within us through our own arrogant rebellion.

Whichever source of temptation you believe in, from the beginning there has been a rebellious dysfunction in the human spirit that has caused people to be "sinful" and "at outs" with God. The Incarnation was God's work of love to give the light of revelation in living example in Jesus to seek to gain the trust of sinful people so the Holy Spirit could lead them to repentant transformation of life and bring them by grace into fellowship with God. That's what I believe the "new birth" (birth from above) described by Jesus to Nicodemus in John 3:1-7 is all about.

Now, having examined three ways Jesus could have approached his work, allow me to share my thoughts about how he chose to do his transforming and reconciling mission among humanity.

Paul was truly inspired when he wrote that it was the great God of all beginnings who revealed himself in the incarnate Jesus: "For it is the God who said, 'Let light shine out of darkness' who has shone in our hearts to give the light of the knowledge of the glory of God in the face of Christ" (2 Cor. 4:6). And from the example of Jesus' life and the inspiration of the Holy Spirit, Paul was led to write that the "fruit of the Spirit is love, joy, peace, patience, kindness, goodness, faithfulness, gentleness, self-control" (Gal. 5:22-23).

In other words, when the Holy Spirit is a guiding, transforming, helping reality in one's life, these are the moral and personal qualities and values that will manifest themselves. This is not about just following a good moral example, but about believing, having faith, and responding to God in terms of a dynamic, life-changing, transforming, new birth from above—a conversion; a grace-wrought, repentant turn from sin to trust in God who is seeking to reclaim and reconcile.

Jesus put a new face on the character of God. The Heavenly Father revealed by Jesus is not a favor-granting or chastisement-meting king. He is not a revenge-seeking, justice-demanding judge. His character is in its essence "caring love" (Greek agape) and "unselfish kindness" (Hebrew hesedh). His highest purpose and his unending ongoing efforts focus on enfolding us in that caring kindness. Before that can happen, however, a "new birth" / "new creation" transformation must come to pass as a reality in a person's life. The closing line of Psalm 23 should read, "Surely, goodness and mercy shall pursue me all the days of my life." That is God's unending search of love for us.

This is what Jesus revealed, taught, and practiced. It was so unacceptable to the Jewish leadership and so threatening to their religious positions, they soundly rejected him and determined that he had to be eliminated to remove his threat to them. To them he was a blasphemer, misrepresenting God and leading the guileless masses astray. So, they manipulated his death. Pilate cared not a whit about their religious scrap, but he would not ignore their threat to "rat him out" to the emperor, so he gave in to their intimidation and "crucified another Jew."

Now, I know this is a different story than that the death of Jesus on Golgotha was an atoning blood ritual sacrifice to "cover over" and "hide from God's eyes" the despicable horror of human sin, but remember that the Bible is filled with metaphorical and figurative language. Jesus used parables, similitudes, and other figurative but deeply meaningful forms of teaching. The theological doctrine that Jesus was designed in eternity to be the "Lamb of God crucified from the foundation of the world" came from other sources, not from the life and teachings of Jesus as recorded in the Gospels. Jesus did not seek to "reconcile and create harmony" by following the way of power to make people obey.

We are not saved by something someone outside us does for us or to us. We are saved from our self-centeredness and arrogance by trusting the gracious God to forgive us and work a grace-giving, life-changing, transforming conversion in our very souls. This involves trust on our part and a work of divine grace on God's part. But that is what turns an out-of-sync relationship into an in-sync relationship, and alienation into reconciliation.

Jesus died because from the beginning of his public ministry he settled the matter. He would not bribe people with free food; he would not awe them with wonder-working; he would not try to control them with authority and make them shape up. He came to reveal the true character of God and win the hearts of people to trust God, embrace love, and live in reconciled fellowship with the gracious God whose whole heart of love longs to have all his prodigal children home in his family.

The world killed Jesus for revealing new light they had not seen before. They killed him for revealing a new character of God and a new meaning for religion that was different from the way they had been taught to relate to God. He will bring us to eternal abundant life if we will, as he preached, "repent and believe in the gospel" (Mark 1:14-15). That is personal conversion, and there is no ritual that can accomplish it for us.

This extensive "aside," concerning the experience of Jesus alone in the wilderness at the beginning of his public ministry, is my attempt to present what I understand to be a revealing parallel. The three features of the wilderness testing reflect the traditions of human responses to the ministry events recorded in the Gospels. The testing was not about personal temptations to Jesus but about his divinely insightful knowledge about human nature and about what would save sinners from perishing in alienation from God, by reconciling them into "born from above, new creatures in Christ" living "abundant, eternal life" in trust and harmony with God.

...

NOTES

[1] S. Maclean Gilmour, "Luke's Special Tradition," *The Interpreter's Bible*, vol. 8 (New York: Abingdon, 1952), 14-15. Bible Iliad, "The Structure of Matthew" and "Major Themes in the Gospel of Luke," www.umass.edu/wsp/alpha/iliad/matthew.html (accessed Mar. 4, 2019).

[2] William Barclay, *The Gospel of Luke*, 2nd ed. (Philadelphia: Westminster, 1956), 38.

[3] Eugene H. Peterson, *The Message* (Colorado Springs, CO: NavPress, 2005), 1670.

[4] William F. Arndt and F. Wilbur Gingrich, trans., Walter Bauer's *Greek-English Lexicon of the New Testament*, 2nd ed. (Chicago: University of Chicago Press, 1979), 219a.

Ministry in Galilee

(Luke 4:14–9:50)

THE BEGINNING OF PUBLIC MINISTRY

(4:14-15)

According to the Synoptic Gospels, after his baptism and temptations in the Judean area in the Jordan Valley near its flow into the Dead Sea, Jesus moves from Judea to Galilee. The Fourth Gospel includes stories of a more expanded ministry in Judea before the movement to Galilee. Luke 4:14 simply records that Jesus begins his teaching ministry, whereas both Matthew (4:17) and Mark (1:15) record the central content of his preaching/teaching: Repent, and believe the gospel, for the kingdom of God/heaven has drawn near.

REJECTION AT NAZARETH

(4:16-30)

Jesus begins his ministry by going into local synagogues and teaching. The first record of his synagogue teaching is about a visit on the Sabbath to his hometown of Nazareth.

The Tabernacle/Temple had been the holy center of Jewish religion since the time of Moses. There the Holy of Holies (the representative place of God's presence among them) was located and there the multitudes of priests (sons of Aaron and tribe of Levi), daily and at all Jewish festivals, performed the rituals of burning offerings in sacrifice. That priority focus on the Temple and the ritual sacrifices was maintained until the Babylonians conquered Jerusalem and destroyed the temple in 586 BCE.

The origin of the synagogue is not clearly identified in history, but very possibly came after the Temple was destroyed and the exiles separated from Jerusalem and their Temple during the Babylonian Exile. The synagogue was not a place for ritual sacrifices and offerings, but rather a teaching institution to preserve the Torah (Mosaic Law), teach it to the people, and give religious impetus to the ongoing practice of the Mosaic teachings. In the synagogue a rabbi, or visiting religious teacher, would read from a sacred scroll and give a homily (sermon/lesson) from the passage read.

Jesus has already developed a reputation as a teacher (he was often addressed as "Rabbi" or "Rabboni," both meaning "teacher"), so when he comes to the synagogue he is called on to be the reader/teacher for the day. When handed the scroll of Isaiah, he follows the practice of standing to read the passage. He goes to the passage that in our Old Testament is chapter 61, verses 1-2, except that the record in Luke has him omit a final statement: "the day of vengeance of our God."

We do not know if Jesus actually omitted the reference to vengeance or if in the years of tradition before Luke recorded it, that statement had been dropped off. In his life and teaching Jesus made almost no reference to any "vengeance" in the heart of God, and he gave new meaning to many of the ritual regulations of the developed Mosaic religious system.

The passage follows the tradition of the Servant Songs in Second/Third Isaiah (the captivity and return periods) about the mission of Israel as God's servant. It reflects two different streams of thought in the developing messianic hope:

1. God will raise up a powerful military leader to vanquish enemies and elevate Israel to world dominance.
2. God will raise up an anointed spiritual leader who will make central the values of God to meet human need and uplift human life.

Jesus says that God's purpose is fulfilled in him (v. 21), and that purpose is a spiritual and human uplift. This emphasis by Jesus supports the Lukan tradition that Jesus, by his life and teaching, both practices and commissions care for the outcast and underprivileged in society.

The response of the crowd to Jesus' teaching is divided. Some say, "He can't do anything special; he is just a hometown boy, son of a carpenter" ("No prophet is acceptable in his own country," v. 24). Others say, "If he can do the kind of things we have heard about him doing in Capernaum, why doesn't he do them here for us?" Jesus replies that God is doing wondrous things among Gentiles as well as Jews (ex.: a widow in Sidon in Phoenicia, and Naaman the leper from Syria). His answer offends his Jewish neighbors and they try to "throw him out of town," but in the chaos he just goes quietly away.

MINISTRY IN CAPERNAUM
(4:31-37)

After being thrown out of Nazareth, Capernaum becomes the nearest thing to a hometown Jesus has. The people there are astounded at his teaching. It has the quality of authority, but is quite different from the Hebrew religion they have been taught all their lives.

In the synagogue at Capernaum Jesus heals a man who is demon-possessed. Remember that in his day people thought mental illnesses were caused by divine chastisement or demon possession (see John 9:2-3). The Gospels record that Jesus effectively heals both physical and mental illnesses and declares that chastisement for sin is not a cause.

Also, note how many of the incidents in the interrelation of Jesus and the crowds parallel and throw light on the struggle for a course to follow (called "temptations") that Jesus had chosen in the wilderness. Although Jesus can give the crowds something they desire (bread to eat or healing from illness), that does not change their hearts and transform their lives. He can awe them with his wonder-working actions (feed a crowd with just a little food or heal illnesses that are incurable by standard treatments of the time), but that does not make them different people afterward.

In the Gospel of John many of these and similar actions by Jesus are described as "signs," indicating who Jesus is—the divine Son of God—but the crowds just bring more sick people to be healed and follow Jesus, hoping for more bread. They do not understand; they do not see the "signs." They spread the word about the amazing things he does, but not so much about the life-changing truths he teaches.

MEETING HUMAN NEEDS
(4:38-44)

Wherever Jesus goes, he meets human needs with deeds of helping kindness. He heals Simon Peter's mother-in-law and numerous other people, and when he starts to leave town to go away alone, the people try to stop him. Jesus says he must go on to preach in other places. Although he does many works such as healing and feeding crowds to answer human needs, his focus is on teaching to reveal life-changing truth to fulfill the purpose of his incarnation.

...

As you read and study the Bible, pay attention to the times Jesus has to help people unlearn what they have been taught about God and religion in Judaism. The Jews had made great leaps in their understanding and beliefs through twenty centuries, but a lot of misunderstanding and other baggage had gotten into the practices of Judaism. Jesus put a new face on God, and he gave radically different and new meaning to the purpose and practice of authentic religion. This is not to discount Judaism as a religion, for Judaism has continued to evolve and modern Judaism is more a morality religion in covenant with God instead of a blood sacrifice ritual religion as Moses started it. The great insight of Micah 6:8 to act justly, love mercy, and walk humbly with God has won.

...

ATTRACTION TO JESUS' TEACHING
(5:1-11)

At times crowds seek Jesus' teaching, but too often they are drawn away by the "awe" from his "wonderworks." At the start of Luke 5, Jesus is teaching from Simon Peter's boat while people listen from the shore, although little is recorded of the content of his teaching. There follows the story of the unexpected catch of fish after a night of futile netting. Here again the focus of the story shifts immediately to the wonder of what has happened.

Luke records the call of Jesus to the first disciples to follow him and become "fishers of men." Matthew (4:18-22) and Mark (1:16-20) both record that this call to the first four followers happens as soon as Jesus goes to Galilee, but neither Matthew nor Mark records the event described in Luke.

RESPONSE TO TRAGEDY AND FEAR
(5:12-26)

Luke 5 records two incidents of healing: those of a leper and a paralyzed man. With leprosy believed to be both contagious and incurable, requiring lepers to live in isolation away from family and outside any community except for other lepers, the man in this story asks Jesus if he is willing to heal a leper. The man's low esteem of his worth reflects the absolute shunning in his culture. Jesus affirms this man's worth, touches him to heal him (a move totally unheard of), and sends him to make an offering for his cleansing. A priest is required to certify him healed and ritually clean before he can go back into the city, to his home and family, and to be in touch with other people.

The story of the healing of a paralyzed man records how religious leaders follow Jesus to "check out" his teaching. They criticize every variance Jesus makes from the details of the Mosaic Law in all the complex interpretations that have developed through the centuries. The story also reflects how the people have already latched on to the awesome idea that Jesus will "heal" all kinds of mental and physical illnesses.

As Jesus attempts to teach, the crowds come with their sick as they seek healing. When Jesus speaks of forgiving sins the scribes accuse him of blasphemy. The question about whether forgiving or healing is "easier to say" (v. 23) refers to that which can be proved. The scribes can deny Jesus' ability to forgive, but if the paralyzed man gets up and walks away, they cannot deny a healing. The crowds respond, not with concerns about Jesus' teaching but with wonder-struck amazement.

CALLING A TAX COLLECTOR
(5:27-32)

Luke records the call of Levi (Matthew) by Jesus. Then Levi invites Jesus to a meal where his tax collector associates (publicans) are gathered. These people are scorned by the citizens because they work as contractors for the Roman government and are considered traitors to their Jewish heritage. Because of their avoidance by fellow Jews, the tax collectors tend to largely associate in groups.

The Pharisees criticize Jesus for his association with these "sinners," but Jesus declares that he has come to call sinners to repentance. There seems to be a couched reference in "the well who have no need of a physician" to the fact that all are sinners in need of repentance. The self-righteous Pharisees have no grounds for their scorn of the tax collectors.

QUESTIONS ABOUT FASTING
(5:33-39)

The questioning of Jesus' motives by the Pharisees and scribes continues around the topic of fasting, again a sign that the meaning of religion to Jesus contrasts with the developed religion of Judaism. Fasting (and sack cloth and ashes) has developed among Jews as a means to reflect how morbidly sad the people consider their guilty selves. Jesus, on the other hand, expresses a joyful celebration about the goodness of life that God offers through forgiveness and abundant life.

The new meaning of faith and grace instead of law and ritual needs new approaches in life to fulfill it. Jesus teaches the people: Don't sew a patch of new cloth on an old garment; it won't turn out well. Don't put new wine into skins that have already been stretched to their limit by previous fermentation. Jesus clearly presents a new revelation about the character of God, the meaning of religion, and the purpose of religious rituals. He concludes with a statement about preferring the old as better, apparently a reference to the Pharisees who are still deeply convinced of the rightness of their devotion to law and ritual.

Jesus' response to his opponents' questions about fasting is in character with what Jesus said in the Sermon on the Mount, "I have not come to abolish [the law and the prophets] but to fulfill them" (Matt. 5:17). The Book of Hebrews begins with the declaration that "In many and varied ways God spoke of old to our fathers by the prophets, but in these last days he has spoken to us by a son" (1:1). Jesus, by incarnate life, revealed that God was giving a new and fuller truth about himself and how he would have us respond to, believe, trust, and follow him.

PROPER CONDUCT ON THE SABBATH
(6:1-11)

Some Pharisees raise a question about the disciples eating grain on the Sabbath and about Jesus healing a man's withered hand in the synagogue on the Sabbath. The people are burdened by the many prohibitions about what they cannot do on the Sabbath. Although the fourth of the Ten Commandments simply states, "Remember the Sabbath to keep it holy," through the years the priests and scribes have added hundreds of "things you must not do" if you are to obey the Sabbath commandment.

Jesus says that eating if you are hungry is more important than not eating just to fulfill some idea about ritual uncleanness *and* that helping a handicapped man is better than neglecting to help him, even if it is the Sabbath and you are in the synagogue. He makes a telling statement in the words, "The Son of Man is lord of the Sabbath." (Mark 2:27 records, "The Sabbath was made for man, not man for the Sabbath.")

In Exodus 20:11 the reason for resting on the Sabbath is to follow the example of God who rested after creating the universe. Deuteronomy 5:15, by contrast, declares that celebration of deliverance from Egyptian bondage in the Exodus is the reason for keeping the Sabbath. In other scriptures Jesus notes, "You have heard it said . . . but I say unto you."

Jesus as much as says, "I know what the Sabbath is all about, and I know what fits into its true meaning." His statements, however, do not in any sense convince and satisfy his critics. They are so deeply offended by Jesus, they are already thinking of ways to stop his teaching and actions.

The Sabbath healing reveals how deeply suspicious the Jewish religious leaders are of Jesus, following him around, trying to find some word or action they can use to convince the people he is a blasphemer, a fraud, and a false prophet. Jesus puts a test to his critics: "Is it lawful on the Sabbath to do good or to do harm?" He heals the man, demonstrates his answer, and refutes their criticism.

CALL OF THE TWELVE DISCIPLES
(6:12-16)

Jesus' action to commission an inner circle of followers is recorded in all three Synoptic Gospels, but at different places in the sequence of events and with minor variations of names that seem fairly well reconcilable. These followers are sometimes called disciples, sometimes apostles, and sometimes just the Twelve. They are the closest and most constant followers of Jesus throughout his public ministry. They are highly esteemed and will play a vital role in the development of the Christian movement.

TEACHINGS BY JESUS
(6:17-49)

Some sections of the Gospels are narratives about where Jesus goes and what he does. As crowds gather around him, Jesus meets needs such as healing the sick and feeding crowds. The people then focus on his wonder-works more than on his teachings.

Luke presents a section of teaching that parallels part of the Sermon on the Mount found in Matthew 5–7, with Luke's tradition from the Gentile Asia Minor area and Matthew's from the Jewish Palestine area reflected in the differences between the two Gospel accounts.

In the Beatitudes (6:20-23) Luke has "poor" instead of "poor in spirit" and "hunger" instead of "hunger and thirst after righteousness." Statements such as these are basic to the widely held belief that Luke reveals a special identification by Jesus with the down-trodden, abused, and most needy groups in human society. Luke does not include the "meek," "merciful," "pure in heart," and "peacemaker" beatitudes. He expands the persecution and conflict with other beatitudes and includes four woes (vv. 24-26) Matthew does not have. The Lord's Prayer, which Matthew includes in the Sermon on the Mount, Luke includes in a shorter version at a different place (11:1-4) in response to the disciples asking him to teach them to pray.

The "love your enemies" section (6:27-31) raises the question about how can we measure up to such an ideal. To understand the meaning of "love" here, we need to distinguish between the meanings of Greek words in contrast to our English usage of words. The Greek text has *agape*, not *philia*. *Agape* refers to the love of God toward humanity—unselfish, outwardly focused, compassionate care. *Philia*, on the other hand, refers to friendship—as in choosing to be friends with people you like. "Love your enemies," therefore, means to care about them in appropriate ways as we are able and as they are willing to be helped.

The admonition to love our enemies also comes into play in the question of adversaries in warfare, but here Jesus is talking about interpersonal relations person-to-person—not about nations at war. He makes this distinction in the next passage (vv. 32-36), where he focuses on motivations, on what we expect back in return from how we relate to others. Do we love those who love us so we will be loved? Do we help others so they will return the favor with a margin of benefit for us?

Jesus teaches us that to be like God we have to be different from people whose motivation is always to get back more than they give. Jesus points out that God is "kind to the ungrateful and selfish," so we have to be merciful even to people from whom we expect unkindness if we would be like God.

...

Here the question of the meaning of "holy" helps us. The root concept behind the word "holy" is "other" (different). God is holy. That means he is "other" than we are. He is infinite; we are finite. He is all powerful; we are limited in what we can do. He is all knowing; we are limited in our ability to know. He is everywhere-present; we are limited by time and space and matter in a physical world. The "awesome otherness" of God is what the Bible means when it says that God is "holy." And, of course, we have a clear admonition in the Bible, "You shall be holy, for I am holy" (1 Pet. 1:16).

It is true that holiness is generally thought of as referring to an exalted quality of moral life, which is not inaccurate. But holiness in the Christian life should mean the difference, the otherness in our lives that results from our faith. When we "believe the gospel" and repent, when we change our minds about God and ourselves, when we choose to change our values because we trust God, when we therefore choose to change the actions of our lives so that by God's grace we can live in harmony with him in reconciled fellowship—then we become changed persons and unlike people who live by another set of values and a different relationship with God. Call it "being born again from above."

...

The paragraph about judging (6:37-38) also deals with how we treat others in interpersonal relationships. Jesus points out that we tend to get back what we give, that we treat each other like we are treated. Human relations are too often and too much a get-even way of life. We praise its instruction but too often fail to treat others the way we would like to be treated per the Golden Rule.

The following paragraph (vv. 39-42) is called a parable, but it seems not so much a parable as a group of examples about how people relate to each other in their daily lives. We tend to want more competence from those who can help us than we have in our area of need. If we are blind, we need someone who can see. If we want to learn, we need someone who has advanced more in that area than we have. But then we turn things around, trying to help someone else with a problem while we have not dealt with bigger problems of our own (sawdust in their eyes, and logs in our own). We want from others more than we are willing or prepared to give. Life is indeed filled with spiritual challenges if we try to follow Jesus and become more like him.

Jesus then uses trees and fruit to illustrate the relationship of truth and reality (vv. 43-45). The quality of a tree determines the quality of fruit it will bear, and the fruit of the tree reveals the quality of the tree. Truth and reality go together, and to pretend or claim otherwise is utter folly that will be inescapably exposed in the end.

...

In this matter I am convinced that the Christian movement has erred grievously. In areas such as church membership, baptism, the Lord's Supper and ordination, some of the historic teachings of the churches have encouraged people to believe that these practices have given them something in their relationship with God that they do not in reality have. Jesus asked forthrightly, "Why do you call me Lord, and do not what I tell you?" Every generation has known too many clear examples that expose the unreality of religious vows and claims in the lives of tragic personal failures. The fruit of a tree does indeed reveal the nature of the tree. Church membership, baptism, communion, and ordination have true value when they are the "fruit" of authentic reality in a person's living relationship with God.

...

Luke concludes this section of teaching (vv. 46-49) with the same examples of houses and foundations and outcomes that Matthew (7:24-27) places at the end the Sermon on the Mount. Jesus asks his hearers whether there is any meaning to their addressing him as "Lord." In their culture the title "Lord" implies established and recognized authority, and authority is meant to be obeyed. So, hearing words should be followed by action if the words have any meaning. Jesus goes on to teach a lesson about foundations and houses. The ability of a house to stand the tests of time depends on the sturdiness of its foundation. No matter how good the structure, without a solid foundation the house will not last. Calling Jesus "Lord" has meaning only when we live faithfully in our relationship with him.

HEALING OF THE CENTURION'S SERVANT
(7:1-10)

A Roman centurion army officer (and a Gentile), who commands a hundred soldiers, has a critically ill slave. Having heard about Jesus' healing activity, he asks his Jewish acquaintances to make a request to Jesus on his behalf. (Matt. 8:5 reads that the centurion himself comes and makes the request.) The Jews comply with the request, describing the centurion as one who is worthy to receive the favor because he has helped those in his area of occupation with the construction of a synagogue. Jesus agrees to go with them to the centurion's house.

Before the group reaches the house, however, the centurion sends other "friends" (the record does not indicate if these were Jews or not). Their message is about authority and what is expected of it. The centurion says, "You don't have to trouble yourself. I recognize authority. Just say the word and what you command will happen." Jesus tells the people with him that this is an outstanding example of faith. When the centurion returns to the house, the sick slave is well. Interestingly, this healing happens in Capernaum and involves a Gentile *and* away from the actual presence of Jesus. (A similar story about healing a person at a distance is recorded in John 4:46-53.)

HEALING OF THE WIDOW'S SON
(7:11-17)

A crowd follows Jesus as he travels from Capernaum to Nain, a town located twenty miles southwest of Capernaum and five miles southeast of Nazareth. Near the town's gate Jesus and the crowd meet a funeral procession headed to a burial place for a young man. (This is likely on the day of death because of Jewish belief in the ritual uncleanness of dead bodies, leading to requirements that the dead be buried as quickly as possible [see Num. 5:2]).

Jesus speaks comfort to the young man's mother, then tells the dead man to arise—and gives him back to his mother. Fear seizes the people (v. 16), not as terror about Jesus but as awe in his presence, for they glorify God and talk about God being present and active among them through Jesus. Nothing is told about his life after his restoration nor about his later second death. No doubt this incident raises the curiosity of people who are focused more on Jesus as a wonder-worker than as a teacher.

THE LAST EXCHANGE BETWEEN JESUS AND JOHN
(7:18-35)

Through the revelations Jesus is making by his incarnate life and teaching and practice, significant changes in religious understanding and practice are coming about. John's disciples report on the work of Jesus to John, who is confined to prison, so John sends messengers to inquire of Jesus: "Are you he who is to come, or shall we look for another?" (v. 19).

John is a transitional person. He is a "before Jesus" Jew, steeped in the beliefs about God and the meaning of religious practices reflected in the Hebrew Scriptures. He is familiar with the Hebrew practice of immersion (baptism) as a washing to cleanse the effects of Gentile uncleanness because of "ignorance and alienation from the life of God" (Eph. 4:17-19). John has come to believe, as the prophets Amos (5:24) and Micah (6:8) preached, that God requires high morality in life and not just sacrificial and ritual obedience in the practice of religion. John requires of those who come to him for baptism that they "bring forth the fruits of repentance" before baptism (Luke 3:7-20).

John is also steeped in the Hebrew messianic hope for God to raise up a new divinely anointed son of David who as a great king and military leader will drive out the hated occupying Romans and restore the fortunes of national Israel to prosperity and prominence. When Jesus shows no indication of fulfilling that hope, but rather damps down any hints that people want to "make him a king," John has to question what is going on.

Jesus' reply to John reflects a transition from the type of teaching by John to that of Jesus: Look at what I am doing and learn from it. After John's messengers leave, Jesus describes John as a signal person in the developing meaning of religion. He is indeed a prophet in the pattern of Hebrew prophets, but he is also a "forerunner" for the coming of the incarnation and ministry of Jesus. The Pharisees do not accept John's message (vv. 29-30). Jesus replies that, as different as he and John are—John being an ascetic, and Jesus a celebrator of life)—the Jewish religious leaders have summarily rejected them both.

Unselfish helpfulness to others because of caring kindness lies at the heart of true goodness as a basic moral value in the world. The true purpose of faith and religious practices is not to influence God through rituals so as to assuage his wrath for human disobedience and to gain his forgiveness and favors. Rather, the true purpose of faith and religious practices is to bring transformation to the inner soul of a person and reconciliation with God. That transformation can come only by authentic repentance that begins with genuine trust in the God whose inherent nature is *agape*.

Jesus in his incarnation is indeed putting a new face on God and a new meaning on religion. The eighth-century prophets (Isaiah, Hosea, Amos, Micah) reflect a beginning of that new way of understanding the character of God and the meaning of religion, and Jesus gives it a "full flower" of revelation.

THE ANOINTING OF JESUS
(7:36-50)

The anointing of Jesus is a revealing story that needs comparative examination. We find a similar story in Matthew (26:6-13) and Mark (14:3-9), but they are very different. In the Matthew and Mark accounts the man is named Simon and identified as a leper. In the Luke account he is named Simon and identified as a Pharisee.

In the Matthew and Mark accounts the setting is in Bethany during the last days before the Crucifixion and the woman is not named, but she is traditionally identified as Mary of the Lazarus and Martha family (I assume from the Bethany location). In the Luke account the story has no time or place indication, so we do not know when in the sequence of events or where it occurs, and the woman is identified as "a woman of the city, a sinner" (usually thought to be a prostitute).

In the Matthew account the disciples complain about the "waste" of the valuable ointment that could be given to the poor. In the Luke account the complainers voice concern about Jesus allowing the sinful woman to touch him (thinking of this as a ritual defiling of Jesus, and being considered by the host as an insult to him to let this happen in his house).

In the Matthew and Mark accounts Jesus responds that the woman has done the anointing because she is sensitive to the critical situation caused by the rabid opposition to Jesus in Jerusalem (next door to Bethany). Jesus says the anointing is in fact an "anointing beforehand for his burial." In the Luke account Jesus tells a parable to Simon about forgiveness and grateful love and identifies the anointing and foot washing as an expression of that grateful love by a sinner who has experienced forgiveness. He gives affirmation to the woman about faith, forgiveness, and peace.

This incident from the life of Jesus reflects some clear indications about the meaning of religion. To Simon, religion means careful obedience to the established Mosaic regulations of ritual faithfulness. Nothing in his religious perspective causes him to have compassion for the woman who may well have been forced into prostitution for survival, as the Jewish culture of the day has no provisions for women without a father or husband except begging for charity.

Simon's religious experience has not had a transforming effect on his life. He is rigidly self-righteous and evidently has no understanding of the meaning of forgiveness nor sensitivity to or care about the long-established practice of hospitality to anyone, including strangers, who come into one's house.

The woman, on the other hand, has experienced the scorn heaped upon her by a harshly critical society. She had earlier observed Jesus in his care for people's needs and his apparent willingness to help human recovery from depraved living and offer forgiveness freely. She has come to trust something in Jesus that makes her want to express her gratitude to him. Jesus interprets her action to Simon as an act of love. In the concluding verse Jesus clearly joins faith with a transforming change in life and the beatitude that comes from forgiveness and conversion.

THE ROLE OF WOMEN

(8:1-3)

Luke 8 highlights the important role of women in the ministry life of Jesus. Women support the Twelve, which relieves the disciples of dependence on day-to-day hospitality along their travels. (There is no indication of the source of the women's wealth.) They are a diverse group. Mary Magdalene had a tragic past before her healing from demon possession. Joanna is a prominent lady, the wife of a government official. Susanna and others (not named) are recipients of ministry by Jesus, and now they are devoted followers of Jesus. William Barclay writes that the diversity among them is no hindrance to their acceptance of each other, nor to their working together in their shared mission.[1]

Although treated as subordinate in patriarchal cultures, women were vitally important as supporters. Some were significant decision-makers as leaders in family life and public actions, for example: Sarah chose between Ishmael and Isaac (Gen. 21:8-11). Rebekah chose between Esau and Jacob (Gen. 27:1-35). Bathsheba insisted on crowning Solomon instead of Adonijah as king (1 Kgs. 1:15-31). And, Anna was an early voice of praise for the infant Jesus (Luke 2:36-38).

Christian history is replete with examples of faithful women who have served and led. Churches are enhanced and strengthened by the gifts and commitments of devoted women who sense a call to ministry in Christian service.

THE PARABLE OF THE SOWER
(8:4-15)

The disciples ask Jesus the meaning of a parable he tells about a sower, the seed he sows, and the different soils the seed falls upon. More expansive accounts of the parable are found in Matthew (13:1-9) and Mark (4:1-9), while Luke's is the briefest account. The three parallel passages raise a troubling question.

Jesus seems to be saying that parables are used so that some hearers will be helped to understand truths about the kingdom of God while other hearers will be prevented from grasping these truths. In responding to the disciples' request for the meaning of the parable, Jesus uses metaphorical teaching:

• The seed represents the word of God.
• The kinds of soil represent the hearts and lives of people who hear the word of God, the responses they make, and consequences of those responses.
• The soil of the path is hard-packed and represents hard-hearted people who have no spiritual interest, so they slough off the spiritual message and let it have no place in their hearts and no influence in their lives.
• The thin soil that lies on bedrock represents people who give a quick affirmative response to the word of God when they hear it, but who do not have the depth of commitment that will enable them to stay faithful in times of distraction or trouble or temptation.
• Soil that is full of weeds and bushes represents people whose lives are so filled with pursuing "stuff," pleasures, and the passing values of this life that they have no time and not enough concern about the "things of God" so the "word of God" gets "choked out" and cannot produce any fruit in life.

• The good soil represents people who hear the word of God as "good news," who embrace it with a response of faith and trust in God that is manifest in richly fruitful lives. (Matthew and Mark both add statements about thirty, sixty, and hundredfold degrees of fruitfulness that would be indicative of the variable talents and opportunities of different people.)

THE WORTH OF LIGHT
(8:16-18)

After sharing the parable of the sower, Luke briefly includes a statement from Jesus about how we use light, i.e. to make it possible to see (Matt. 5:15, Mark 4:21-25). These verses seem to confirm that Jesus does not mean in verses 9-10 that parables are used to keep some people from understanding and accepting the spiritual truths being taught.

JESUS AND HIS FAMILY
(8:19-21)

Luke seems to present a more positive concern by Jesus for his physical family than do the Gospel parallels (Matt. 12:46-50, Mark 3:31-35). In verse 21 he is not devaluing his physical family but is affirming the reality of bonding in spiritual relationships for those who share a common commitment to God (what the early church later calls "koinonia").

THE STILLING OF A STORM
(8:22-25)

All three Synoptic Gospels record the stilling of a storm. Luke gives no indication of the time or place in the sequence of other events. This is one of Luke's many "one day" items, or events that his tradition does not give context for but that are too authentic and too important to not include.

The Sea of Galilee is a fresh water lake in the Jordan River valley and lies in a bowl of surrounding mountains. The effects of the rising or falling of air on the slopes of the mountains means that often a storm can arise in only a brief time, creating waves that could endanger small boats. Such is the situation described in these verses. The disciples are frightened, for they are familiar with that sea and its storms. Jesus speaks words of peace to the winds, giving assurance to the disciples as the winds die down and the sea calms.

A "MADMAN" AND SOME PIGS
(8:26-39)

Matthew (8:28-34), Mark (6:1-20), and Luke (8:26-39) all have accounts of a mad man whom Jesus heals. Their records have the same essential factors in the story, but there are sufficient differences that reflect their varying traditions. Remember that in the primitive past, mental illness was believed to be demon-possession. Affected by lack of scientific information, ancient people were consequently vulnerable to superstition. The Gospel writers apparently took some nucleus of an actual event and made it into expanded folklore:

A well-known, mentally-ill man rages across the countryside when he sees people in the vicinity. On this occasion, by his raging, he frightens the swine into such panic that they dash away from him into the sea. Jesus, by his insight into the nature of the man's distress, and by his compassion for anyone whose life is in troubled turmoil, is able to calm the man and help him to recover some order in his life. It's not far-fetched to call it a healing, and even a miracle. The crowds who witness this event have no comprehension of what has happened because of their belief in demon-possession; they want Jesus to go away. Then, Jesus sends the man home with an account of his recovery so he can be reestablished with his family from whom he has been alienated by his mad behavior.

TWO HEALINGS
(8:40-56)

A synagogue official entreats Jesus to heal his seriously ill daughter. On the way to Jairus' house a woman, who has long suffered from hemorrhaging that no one has been able to heal, comes into the crowd and takes hold of Jesus' clothing. She has faith that such an act of faith might be her last hope, but at least a hope. Jesus senses what has happened and affirms to her that faith indeed has powerful healing effect in our lives. He gives his blessing to her act of faith.

Word then comes from the home of Jairus that his daughter has died, thinking there is no longer any reason to ask for help from Jesus. Even in the face of death Jesus assures the child's parents and his closest followers that all hope is not lost. They all go into the room where the young lass is. The group is incredulous as Jesus restores the girl to active life.

...

The events in Luke 8:22-56 reflect how much of the surviving traditions preserved in the Gospels focus on "wonderworks" and "healings." Apparently the crowds who follow Jesus are more impressed by the supernatural things he does than they are by the teachings about God and life that he indicates are the focus of his mission among them.

...

A MINISTRY AND TRAINING PROJECT
(9:1-15)

When Jesus sends the Twelve out (Mark 6:7 says two by two) to preach and heal, he tells them not to take food, clothing, or money for support but to rely on the hospitality of people in the places they go, And, if they do not receive acceptance and hospitality, they are to "shake off the dust" and go on to other places. (This passage undergirds my conviction that the gift of free will means that grace is freely offered, but the choice of whether to trust and accept it is ours.)

Luke includes an account of the turmoil Herod has after his execution of John the Baptist at the request of Herodias and Salome (see Mark 6:14ff). The wonder-working reputation of Jesus has led to speculation that Elijah has come back to life or that John has been raised from the dead. Herod wants to see Jesus and receive an answer to his perplexity.

When the Twelve return from their preaching experience, they tell Jesus how things have gone with them. The group apparently wants to have some time to share the meaning of those events, but they have no time; a crowd follows after them.

While Jesus is engaged in teaching the crowd, human need calls for attention. So, Jesus heals some ill persons and feeds the crowd gathered, using the familiar "five loaves and two fish." Here again, what Jesus does (wonder works) is more impressive, and apparently more important, to the crowd than what he teaches.

...

This story raises an interesting question. In ancient times there were no fast food stops along the wayside. It seems unlikely that crowds of people would have gone away from their homes for extended periods of time without taking food. The fact that a young boy did have a lunch with him seems to indicate that taking food was a customary thing to do. It does not seem unlikely to believe that the people hesitated to begin eating without knowing if any others had food. When the lad was willing to share his lunch, it was enough to persuade the others to share their food so there was more than enough for all.

This possible answer seems to disregard the apparent "miracle" nature in the story. Don't overlook the fact, however, that persuading people to become sharers instead of keeping everything for themselves would have been as surely "miraculous" as if Jesus had "enlarged" the quantity of food to be more than was eaten. Don't ever question what God can do. Just be awed and grateful at God's compassionate kindness and at the amazing ways he works to meet human needs.

...

THE DISCIPLES' CONFESSION OF JESUS AS MESSIAH
(9:18-22)

Luke 9 discloses an incident that Matthew (16:13-23) records as occurring near Caesarea-Philippi. Jesus uses the same ideas that perplexed Herod: Who is Jesus? The people speculate Elijah or John or a prophet, so the disciples reply that this is the talk going around. Jesus then questions: "Who do you say that I am?" Peter answers for the Twelve: "The Messiah"

(God's Anointed One). This confession stands in the biblical records as a signal moment in the growing faith of the disciples in the unique person of Jesus. (Likewise, Jesus' question is a crucial one for every person: "What do you believe about who Jesus is?") Jesus follows up by telling his disciples not to tell this to others. His caution occurs at several places throughout the Gospel records.

By the time Jesus was born, a strong messianic hope had developed among the Jews. Their long-time subjugation to alien empires led to widespread dreaming of a return to the golden age of David. They hoped for a new "son of David" to arise from David's descendants who with "God's anointing" would be a great king who could raise a mighty army and successfully throw off the hated armies of the enemy and restore Israel to prominence and prosperity again.

During the years of Jesus' life there was a constant readiness by a militarist group, the Zealots, to start a "messianic war" at any time. Sometimes, when Jesus did wonder-working things, the crowds wanted "to take him and make him a king." Jesus had not come to be a military revolutionary, and he knew that any such activity would be violently repressed by the Romans, so he "damped down" any messianic demonstrations while he went about teaching and demonstrating the gracious, peaceful, helpful ways of God. God's kingdom is not a geographic area of earthly form, but a spiritual realm of love and peace.

From the time of Peter's confession on behalf of the Twelve, Jesus tells his followers plainly that the violent opposition of the Jewish religious leaders will result in his death. But he assures them he will "be raised" and his death will not be a victory for his opponents, his divine mission prevailing in the end.

...

I believe it is significant that Jesus described the cause of his coming death to be the rejection by the Jewish religious leaders, their violent reaction to the different teaching about and practice of religion he was revealing. I do not find in the Gospel records a description of his death as a "blood-atoning sacrifice" as it is so widely interpreted in traditional Christian theology. That doctrine is found in the New Testament, but it comes from other sources, not Jesus.

...

FOLLOWING JESUS
(9:23-27)

All three of the Synoptic Gospels record this sequence of events: (1) Simon Peter speaks for the disciples and declares their faith that Jesus is their hoped-for Messiah. (2) Jesus begins to tell them he will be rejected by the Jewish religious leaders and killed. (3) Jesus makes it clear that following him will involve a life not centered on personal or present life interests and desires.

The recorded words from Jesus about the Christian life are stark, but I find most interpretations of them to be troubling—especially those regarding his call to deny oneself. In Greek, "to deny" means "to ignore." The grammatical form of the verb refers to something a person is doing to/for himself as an ongoing thing. Most scholars I have studied interpret this to mean that we are to treat ourselves as though we have never existed. I do not agree. Jesus calls on us to love our neighbor as ourselves, not instead of ourselves. I understand that Jesus meant by denying ourselves we are to take selfish personal interests out of the place of first priority and live with a broader soul focused on the will of God, the well-being of others, and the best interests of ourselves.

...

Jesus is recorded in all three Synoptic Gospels as saying that following him involves taking up one's cross. The timing troubles me. According to the time sequences in the Gospels, this event happens before Jesus' last journey to Jerusalem, just after the disciples have affirmed their faith that Jesus is the Messiah, and just as he is beginning to tell them plainly about his coming death. It seems that his reference to bearing a cross would be terribly confusing to the disciples at that time because crucifixion was a Roman means of executing criminals. Reference to taking up one's cross will take on meaning for Christians after the Crucifixion when it becomes a description of what it means to follow the example of Jesus.

A valid question also arises as we try to understand whether or not Jesus really calls us to martyrdom. Or, is a more accurate understanding conveyed by Paul's appeal to "present your bodies as a living sacrifice" (that is, by a life of devoted and selfless service; see Rom. 12:1)? I have to believe that this reference to taking up one's cross was added as the traditions developed through the years. While taking up one's cross is or can be a valid feature of an authentic Christian life, a clear distinction needs to be made. Nothing is a cross except that which causes harsh suffering to you because you are a follower of Jesus and would not have happened to you for any other reason. Most contemporary American Christians have never experienced anything that could by any imagination be called a cross.

The verses after the reference to cross-bearing speak a more applicable word for us from Jesus. His words about "losing life" and "saving life" concern the value choices we make as we live. We live daily in a time, space, and material realm where the needs, desires, pleasantries, and aspirations of physical pleasure, recognition, and security are forever affecting us. But these influences belong entirely to our physical life.

An almost universal belief, however, is that as human persons we are more essentially spiritual in nature, which distinguishes us from the lower species of mere animal creatures. The life values of the spirit are those qualities of character that ultimately make us the kind of persons we are. These qualities of character are wherein we are like the supreme ideal of good or in variance from that ideal. In religion that means whether we are living in harmony and fellowship with God or out of sync with the eternal divine character. The admonition by Jesus is about priority. God raised up human persons to be both physical beings and spiritual persons. I am convinced that one of the basic purposes of our physical life is an opportunity to learn, evaluate, and choose the difference between "the passing" and "the lasting" values of life, and to develop the capacity to keep them in balance by priority choices.

The closing words in the paragraph about "seeing the kingdom of God" raise the important question about the meaning of "the kingdom." The human tendency to materialize everything has led to wide belief in a geographical and material "kingdom" usually identified as Jesus sitting on a throne in Jerusalem and reigning over a new glorious city, or a heavenly paradise with mansions, streets of gold, and evergreen fruit trees. The kingdom of God, as Jesus referred to it, is the "realm where the will of God prevails," and the will of God prevails in the lives of people who trust the wisdom, goodness, grace, and guidance of God, and strive to live in committed harmony with him. That kingdom is spiritual and eternal, and we see it revealed in the lives of people.

...

THE TRANSFIGURATION
(9:28-36)

The transfiguration of Jesus has been variously understood and interpreted. In the Synoptics the text describes a literal change in the countenance of Jesus and the mystical appearance of Moses and Elijah to Peter, James, and John. The event is more than the three apostles can grasp while on the mountain (and more than we can comprehend after all the years of human searching since the death/resurrection of Jesus). The experience is a confirmation to the apostles that their growing faith in Jesus as Messiah is indeed true.

The Transfiguration has been widely understood as figurative, growing out of a dream vision of the apostles or as a throwback of a post-resurrection appearance into the pre-crucifixion records. I believe William Barclay is correct in his contention that we cannot know exactly what happened on that mountain.[2] The described experience is something of which we know nothing. But the story, whatever its actual nature, reveals an awesomely wonderful truth about Jesus. In the Incarnation God came into human experience (see Phil. 2:5-8).

RETURN TO THE WORLD OF HUMAN NEED
(9:37-45)

As soon as Jesus comes down from the mountain to where a crowd is gathered, he is asked to be a wonder-worker and heal an epileptic boy. The boy's father reports that the disciples have not been able to heal his son—his condition thought by the people to be the result of an evil spirit controlling him, a common belief about both physical and mental illness in prescientific times. Jesus commands the evil spirit to leave the boy, which is how the people understand healing.

As usual, the people marvel at the wonder-working by Jesus. But Jesus tells them the important thing at hand is the approaching confrontation with the powerful leaders in Jerusalem who will manipulate his death. His disciples do not grasp the meaning of what he says. The Jews believe that the Messiah will be a victorious military king, so if Jesus is the Messiah, what is he talking about?

THE MOST IMPORTANT?
(9:46-48)

The human tendency to seek recognition and privilege is reflected in the argument by the disciples about who is greatest. (It is also the reason behind many schoolyard scraps between growing boys, a lot of primping by teenage girls, unfettered greed by business moguls, wars, and assassinations of Old Testament kings.) Jesus challenges that attitude about greatness by emphasizing the qualities of humility ("he who is least"), care for others ("receives a child"), and perception of spiritual values ("receives me and him who sent me"). While aspiration for achievement can be a source of human advance, undisciplined ambition can easily lead to arrogance and disregard for the well-being of others.

BELONGING AND NOT BELONGING
(9:49-50)

One of Jesus' closest disciples, John, reports that he and the other disciples have forbidden an exorcist to cast out demons in Jesus' name because the exorcist is not one of their group.

Jesus makes it clear to the disciples that moral and spiritual distinctions are what count with God, for "he who is not against you is for you."

The attitude of the disciples is reminiscent of the ages of polytheism in religion when different tribal groups believed they had a special relation to the deity they worshipped that no one else had. In the cult groups of Greek mystery religions only the "initiated" were allowed into their cult rituals. Even after monotheism became the faith of post-exilic Jews, they still divided the world into the separate Jew/Gentile categories reflected in the Old Testament. Simon Peter in his experience with Cornelius (Acts 10) and Paul during his first missionary journey (Acts 13–14), learned that the Jew/Gentile division of humanity had no standing with God.

NOTES

[1]William Barclay, *The Gospel of Luke* (Philadelphia: Westminster, 1956), 95-96.
[2]Ibid., 124.

Journey to Jerusalem
(Luke 9:51–19:27)

TRAVEL NARRATIVE
(9:51)

Following his ministry in Galilee, Jesus now sets "his face to go to Jerusalem." The climactic end of the Incarnation is approaching. There are occasional narrative passages, but the nature of the recorded text in what is known as "The Travel Narrative" (9:51-19:27) changes. The teachings are not so often interrupted by crowd focus on wonder-working awe because of the help Jesus gives to sick and troubled people in need.

The Travel Narrative includes teaching passages that have no identifiable time or place reference—for example, parables about the good Samaritan, the prodigal son, and the rich young ruler—which could mean the tradition that has come down to Luke includes these teachings. And, because many of the teaching passages do not include time and place references, Luke weaves them into the text before moving on to the final passion narratives.

Note the following brief narrative passages: 9:51, 9:57, 10:38, 13:22, 17:11, 18:31, 18:35, 19:1, and 19:28. The traditional site of the Transfiguration is in northern Galilee, the last place referenced before 9:51. At 10:38 they are in Bethany, just outside Jerusalem. But in 17:11 they are traveling between Samaria and Galilee, so they are either heading north or have been back into Galilee and are heading south again. These narrative references about movement are so sketchy and unrelated to the other records in this extensive section, they are more of a collection of undated materials, too rich and wonderful to leave out.

BELONGING OR NOT BELONGING
(9:52-62)

The question about belonging or not belonging is still part of the graphic human situation for Jesus and his disciples. Jesus is quite willing to stop in a Samaritan village, but the Samaritans will not agree to receive him.

The harsh animosity reflected here dates back to the historical time of the Assyrian conquest of the Northern Kingdom in 722 BCE. There developed so much intermarriage among the Hebrews left in Samaria with neighbors of the Caananite tribes that they became a mixed-race people. The Jews despised them as unfaithful traitors to their Hebrew heritage and would have nothing to do with them. The Samaritans responded in kind, becoming, along with exiles in Syria, what some label as the Ten Lost Tribes of Israel (see Nehemiah 4–6).

In Luke the Zebedee sons (Jesus calls them "sons of thunder" in Mark 3:17) suggest they "call down fire from heaven" to avenge the offense, but Jesus rebukes them, and they just pass on by. Along the way they meet people who vow their devotion to Jesus but find excuses by which they rationalize their inability to follow him.

Jesus declares a maxim that each of us should take seriously: If you are going to start something ("put your hand to the plow"), the only wise course is to look ahead and not back. The expression about being "fit" for the kingdom does not refer to a quality of moral excellence. The word *euthetos* means "ready for use," as in "equipped" or "trained and committed." Jesus is referring to being ready to follow him, in contrast to the men who were not ready.

A TRAINING MISSION FOR SEVENTY
(10:1-20)

In a lengthy passage Luke describes a mission by seventy disciples and teaching by Jesus after they return. The instructions for the seventy are similar to those for the Twelve in a shorter event in Luke 9:1-6, 10. Jesus makes a clear distinction between the outcomes of receiving the gospel message favorably and rejecting it, resulting from personal choices made by the people hearing the gospel. He also makes it clear that the gospel belongs to Gentiles as freely as to Jews.

Jesus declares woes on unrepentant cities where Jesus spends much of his time and ministry: Bethsaida and Capernaum, Jewish towns along the north shore of the Sea of Galilee; and Chorazin, a Jewish village just a short distance north of Capernaum. He compares these cities to Tyre and Sidon, Phoenician Gentile cities thirty and forty-five miles to the northwest where Jesus visits only once. Luke's inclusion of this comparison reflects his emphasis on the universal scope of the gospel. Jew and Gentile alike can embrace the gospel and be blessed by it or reject the gospel and experience the consequences of that rejection. Note the words of Jesus in verse 16, which surely mean "Whosoever will may . . ." It is equally true that whoever chooses to not believe and embrace the gospel will not be required to do so.

In response to the success report of the seventy, Jesus replies, "I saw Satan fall like lightning from heaven," an expression that describes a tradition from much earlier Jewish history that Satan was a "fallen angel" who had been cast out of heaven after he had led a revolt against God (see the poetic reference in Isa. 14:12-20 and the apocalyptic vision in Rev. 12:7-9).[1]

...

I am persuaded that a change in the belief about the origin of evil developed during and after the Babylonian Exile. Prior to that period the Hebrews/Israelites believed in a single source of good and evil, that God favored and blessed those who were obedient and faithful, but was displeased with and chastised those who were disobedient and unfaithful. During the historic time of the Exile the Jews in Babylon/Persia and the Persian Zoroastrians came to believe that good and evil had different sources.

The Hebrew God, Yahweh, and the Persian god, Ahura Mazda (Wise Lord), were the sources of blessing and well-being. An evil demigod Satan/Angra Mainyu (Evil Spirit) was the cause of evil and all distress and suffering.[2] I believe, further, that divine revelation about the source and cause of evil lies in our human misuse of freedom of choice and personal choice of values and conduct that alienate us from harmony and fellowship with God. Jesus seems to have clearly dealt with the question of good or evil choices from the point of view that these are personal choices we make.

...

Since the context of the current passage is about the life-changing results of believing the gospel, Jesus seems to be declaring that evil is defeated by trust in God's grace and repentant reorientation of our values and our lives. He also warns the seventy to not be impressed with themselves by any sense of special powers, for nothing brings more grace into life than a reconciled fellowship with God. To have and to share the light and the welcome of grace is the best of all gifts.

JESUS REVEALS HIS HEART
(10:21-24)

There are many scripture passages that refer to Jesus praying, but few record the content of his prayers. In Luke 10:21 he prays openly and publicly a prayer of gratitude that the truths of the gospel are so simple and forthright that even children can understand them, but people who think themselves wise readily miss these simple truths by reliance on their sense of personal comprehension. In verse 22 Jesus affirms the unity of the Father God and the Incarnate Son, the sameness of the truth being revealed to humanity, and the reality of the revelation being made through the Incarnation. To his disciples Jesus declares the privilege that is theirs to live at this particular time and to associate with him during his incarnate days.

...

Throughout history people have tried to understand deity, but religious history reveals that not even prophets and kings were able to come to an understanding of the character and eternal purpose of God to a degree that approached the revelation Jesus was making of the Loving Father and Gracious Lord who is the Supreme God. That long-developing growth of comprehension through God's helping Spirit is clearly revealed in the documents of our Bible.

...

THE GOOD SAMARITAN
(10:25-37)

The familiar story of the Good Samaritan begins when a religious leader, a lawyer (a specialist in Mosaic Law of rituals and requirements), joins the procession of adversaries to Jesus. Different groups of Jewish religious leaders are constantly trying to outsmart him and discredit him with the crowds who follow him. The conversation leads the lawyer to state an ancient levitical requirement of kindness to neighbors in the familiar words, "You shall love your neighbor as yourself" (Lev. 19:18). Jesus puts the lawyer on the defensive with approval and instruction. The lawyer then asks, "Who is my neighbor?"

(He would likely have answered his own question—as rabbis through the centuries had interpreted the levitical law—"A fellow Israelite," surely, not a Samaritan.)

Jesus exposes his hypocrisy and Jewish exclusiveness by telling the story of a man (no nationality indicated), a victim of violent robbery left lying on the roadside half-dead. Two Jewish religious leaders pass by but do not bother to help him, even though he might be a fellow-Israelite. By contrast a Samaritan, a despised half-breed to most Israelites, takes care of the wounded man.

Then Jesus tests the lawyer with a question, not the lawyer's question about who is his neighbor, but who proves to be a neighbor to the wounded man. The lawyer cannot avoid the obvious answer: "The one who showed mercy on him." Jesus then makes a response that totally devastates the scheming lawyer: "Go and do likewise."

...

The story of the Good Samaritan stands as a clear revelation by Jesus that neither race, nationality, ethnic group, nor class status should be the determiner of how we fulfill the great principle of caring about one another in human relationships. Humanity, need, and kindness are the determining standards that should guide us.

...

A VISIT IN BETHANY
(10:38-42)

When Jesus visits the home of Martha and Mary, Martha proves to be the busy hostess. She wants everything to be "just right." Mary, on the other hand, is more interested in spending time with their guest and listening to his teaching. Martha focuses on showing hospitality and care for others, while Mary focuses on the spiritual nurture of her own life. Martha complains that Mary isn't helping her with what she (Martha) considers most important.

Jesus gives Martha a lesson about priority and timing. He does not say that hospitality and serving food are not important, but that they can be done at other times; hearing the things Jesus teaches can be done only when he is present. Food lasts only until the next meal, but vital truths live on in our hearts and minds and affect our lives permanently.

...

Whenever I read this passage, I am reminded of a small plaque that hung many years ago just inside the back door of the home of my Aunt Clara Belle Austin. It read: "This House Is Clean Enough To Be Healthy—And Messy Enough To Be Lived In." Priority and timing should affect many of the choices we make every day.

...

TEACHING A PRAYER
(11:1-13)

Luke includes a shortened version (11:2-4) of the prayer Jesus teaches his disciples. Matthew's version (6:9-13) is the longer and more familiar one found in the Sermon on the Mount, as though the prayer is a part of Jesus' teaching on that occasion. Luke includes the prayer as if it is given in answer to a request by the disciples.

...

We can learn from this prayer about the priority of our relationship with God, about the awareness we should have of our dependence on God for our needs, and about the vital role forgiveness has in our relationships with God and others. This prayer is a worthy guide for our daily praying.

...

Jesus follows the prayer with examples about prayer. First, he teaches about a man in need and a friend who is not inclined to be bothered with his friend's need. Persistence prevails. He keeps knocking until the friend relents and helps him. Jesus teaches us to keep on asking, keep on seeking, keep on knocking. Jesus also teaches about how ready God is to answer our prayers with blessings. He uses the example of how parents are happy to give good things to their children, comparing the concern of parents with the readiness of God to give the Holy Spirit

...

People tend to be overwhelmed by the idea of God's infinite greatness as the Creator and his infinite wisdom as designer of the universe. Jesus taught that God is also infinitely good as our Heavenly Father of love and grace.

There is a beautiful expression of this character of God in the closing verse of Psalm 23, "Surely, goodness and mercy shall follow me all the days of my life." An alternate translation of RaDaPh ("to follow after") is "to follow after eagerly, to pursue," as in "goodness and mercy shall pursue me, seek after me, all the days of my life."[3] *God is indeed infinitely good, infinitely powerful, and infinitely wise. God desires, yearns for, nothing more than to bless us, if only we will trust him enough to become able to receive his blessing.*

...

HEALING A "POSSESSED" MAN
(11:14-23)

Because the man in this story is unable to speak, he is considered demon-possessed. His healing gives the adversaries a chance to accuse Jesus of being in league with the prince of demons and that this is the source of his power to exorcise (cast out) demons. This is a part of their ongoing attempts to discredit Jesus and to destroy his favor with the crowds.

Jesus shows the inconsistency of their accusation, however: If demonic leaders cast out demons, it reduces the influences of the whole demonic "kingdom." Jesus then casts their accusation back at his adversaries by asking by what power their sons and allies practice exorcism. He concludes that good and evil contradict each other. Those who follow Jesus will live in harmony with him, and whoever does not live in harmony with him is not his follower.

NATURE ABHORS A VACUUM
(11:24-26)

Like their ancestors, the people of Jesus' day believe that demons are evil spirits that invade and control people but that can be exorcised from a person's life. If healing occurs, a vacuum exists. Jesus teaches that this vacuum will be filled with something.

Ancient people objectified inanimate concepts. They thought of life and death as "things" separate and apart from the body, specifically: life comes into the body and a person is alive; death invades the body and drives out life and a person is dead. This belief also comes from the human inability to grasp the concept of "pure spirit."

Ancients believed that all the many deities (gods) were seeking things in which to embody themselves. So, people set up stone pillars or planted trees in their fields and carved idols of wood or stone or metal, trusting that their god would be pleased and therefore would inhabit it and bless them. (See Lev. 26:1 for a prohibition to the Hebrews.)

...

Life will not exist as a moral vacuum. If a person tries to overcome a bad habit, there is a vital need to develop a good habit to replace it. If life is not filled with good habits, a person is vulnerable to developing, not just one, but many bad habits. We can only develop good habits by deliberate choice and intent and by daily ongoing cultivation and practice. We live in peril of drifting into bad habits unless we choose the upward life of choosing and practicing good habits.

...

LEARNING AND CHOOSING
(11:27-28)

A woman in the crowd, as an expression to praise Jesus, cries out, "It has to have been a wonderful blessing to be your mother." Jesus responds with a declaration that physical relationships are not as important as spiritual relationships. He does not say that human relationships are not important but is pointing out the tendency of people to place priority on experiences of time, matter, and family while failing to be aware of or of ignoring the importance of relationships with God and values of spirit. To "hear the word (gospel) of God" is a fundamental and unending mission we have from God; and to "keep it" (believe, trust, live by) is the moral and spiritual responsibility of each individual person in relationship to God.

...

Birth status has been honored highly among the "noble born" all through human history. But noble in human terms has been associated with wealth and influence, but has too often had no relation to quality of life or contribution to humankind. Birth determines genetic heritage, but the person one "becomes" will result from the choices and pursuits made by that person in potential who is born.

...

RECOGNIZING WHAT MATTERS
(11:29-32)

Jesus seems to be responding to the prevalent tendency of the crowds gathered around and following him to be more interested in him as a wonder-worker than in the religious, moral, and spiritual teachings he is trying to deliver to them. Often when Jesus is engaged in teaching, he pauses to perform an awe-inspiring act to answer a human need such as a healing. At these times the attention, focus, and interest of the crowd turn immediately and obsessively to the "miracle." Jesus speaks about the prevalent request that he give them "a sign." They obviously want him to do more awesome wonderworks that will prove he is the Messiah and will use supernatural powers to supply their wants and to fulfill their national dreams.

Jesus compares the repentance of Nineveh after Jonah's preaching and the search by the queen of Sheba for the wisdom of Solomon to the inability of the crowds who follow him to recognize the importance of what he is teaching and doing. Luke has Jesus openly and clearly declare himself greater than Jonah or Solomon.

LIGHT, PHYSICAL AND SPIRITUAL
(11:33-36)

Jesus focuses on the importance of human recognition of the purpose and value of light, both physical and spiritual. The subject parallels closely the saying in Matthew (5:14-16) by Jesus about his followers being like light in the world. In this instance he emphasizes the importance of an inherent warning to everyone about carefully searching for accurate truthful information (lighting a lamp) in a quest for our "whole body (entire life) to be full of light."

THE DANGER OF SELF-DECEPTION
(11:37-54)

Jesus continues in an interchange with some adversary Pharisees and lawyers. The discussion happens when a Pharisee invites Jesus to dine at his house. The host is astonished when Jesus does not follow the requirement of ritual handwashing before eating. Jesus rebukes the Pharisees by describing the hypocrisy of their practice of washing hands instead of cleansing hearts, as in washing the outside of a dish (which shows) instead of cleaning the inside (which holds the food). He calls them foolish for ignoring the truth that the Creator made both hands and hearts. His admonition is to cleanse the heart, for people with clean hearts will care and be careful about clean hands also. The lawyers then complain that Jesus is reproaching them. (Jesus as much as says, "If the shoe fits, wear it.")

There follows a series by Jesus against the Pharisees and lawyers that is similar to a series of woes recorded in Matthew 23. Jesus declares them guilty of strictly following the ritual of the tithe while neglecting the moral matters of justice and love. He rebukes them for arrogant pride while not having integrity in their lives. To the lawyers who complain, Jesus replies by detailing ways they lay requirements on others that they would not fulfill themselves. He ends his woes to them by describing how generations of Jewish religious leaders have harshly treated anyone who differs with them and offers any meaning of religion they do not approve. Jesus declares that the current leaders are following their example and practice. Luke concludes with a record of the growing opposition by the religious leaders against Jesus.

...

We have an incredible capacity to delude ourselves about our motives and values. It is incredibly easy, once we come to accept an idea as valid, to completely miss the contradictions it may include. It is far harder to "unlearn" an outdated idea, once it has been disproved by advances in learning, than it is to learn a new reality. For example, why do we sometimes still think as though the earth is flat? And why do we see the "speck of sawdust" in our neighbor's eye while missing the "log" in our own? The inevitability of our seeing life from inside ourselves is part of the reason we always should carefully guard against missing the broader meanings and values of life.

...

THE DANGER OF FALSE GUIDANCE
(12:1-3)

Following the interchange of Jesus with the religious leaders, Luke records a collection of teachings and admonitions to a crowd of people (a myriad = an unnumbered multitude). First, Jesus warns about religious teachings that can lead astray. The "leaven" of the Pharisees is a figurative reference to their teachings (see Matt. 16:6-12). Jesus describes them here and elsewhere as being hypocritical, of teaching one thing and practicing something else in their living. His words about things hidden being revealed are a declaration that truth will eventually be known and that falsehood, including hypocrisy, will be exposed.

There is inherent here an admonition to examine carefully what we hear or read. For guidance we need a standard for truth against which we can evaluate the "teaching" of those who speak or write or act. We have no more accurate standard than the life and teachings of Jesus as recorded in the Gospels.

WHO, OR WHAT, TO FEAR
(12:4-7)

Jesus next focuses on the priority value that spirit has in contrast with material things, such as our physical bodies. This seems appropriate following the earlier warning about the harm that can come from false teachings. Any harm to our physical life is finished at death, but anything that adversely affects our spiritual life and our relationship with God can last beyond death if it is allowed to alienate us from God.

The references to killing the body and being cast into hell (Gehenna) are graphic warnings for Jews of the day: the occupying Romans will show no mercy to anyone who crosses them. Jesus warns: beware of the Pharisees and their false teachings that lead people astray. He emphasizes the difference between spiritual and material by contrasting people and sparrows. People are more valuable than sparrows because people are spiritual persons and sparrows are beautiful little animals. But God cares for both.

In traditional belief the someone who can "cast into hell" refers to Satan. I believe otherwise. Eugene Peterson paraphrases James 1:14-15 as "We have no one to blame but the leering, seducing flare-up of our own lust."[4] Since we are persons of free will and responsible choice, nothing and no one alienates people from God and "casts into hell" except their own rebellious selves through their choice of the ways of death instead of the ways of life.

CONFESSION AND FORGIVENESS
(12:8-10)

Jesus continues his teaching on fearless confession by speaking about acknowledging him versus denying him and about forgiveness versus blasphemy.

A person is either in harmony and fellowship with God or not. If someone denies a trust relationship with God, it becomes evident that any other claim to belong with God (as in "before the angels") is unreal and hypocritical. There is an inherent warning here to not expect from God at the time of death a miracle that will change a person into one of harmony with God when that person has had no such prior relationship. Adam and Eve had to leave Eden because they no longer belonged in the garden. We ought not to expect to be welcomed into paradise if we do not "belong" there.

The saying about receiving forgiveness or committing an unforgivable blasphemy against the Holy Spirit is difficult to understand. Jesus is clear at times in his declarations about the unity between himself, the Father, and the Spirit. But the distinction made here seems to have no defined basis

---

Stuart Newman in a theology class at Southeastern Seminary described the unforgivable nature of such a blasphemy as "looking at white, knowing it is white, and declaring it to be black." Such would put a person outside a forgivable possibility. But the statement recorded here does not make clear why that would apply to the Spirit and not the Son. I am not aware of any possible explanation except the promise Jesus made in John 14 that after his death/resurrection/ascension his followers would not be left orphaned and abandoned. The Holy Spirit (*Paraclete*) would be the way God would be present with them as Jesus had been the living presence of God (Emmanuel, God with us) during the days of his incarnation. To deny the living presence of the Holy Spirit in a blasphemous way could so cut a person off from any access to God that such a person would be unable to receive forgiveness. Any "unforgivableness" would be in a human inability to receive forgiveness, and not in any lack of gracious outreach of love to offer forgiveness on God's part.

FACING OPPOSITION
(12:11-12)

The disciples are readily aware of the opposition of Jewish religious leaders to Jesus as they have dogged his steps and tried to discredit him throughout his public ministry. Jesus warns the disciples to expect the same kind of treatment since they have followed him, but he encourages them to not be afraid to identify themselves with him and his teachings; he assures them that the Holy Spirit will be God's way of accompanying and guiding them.

THE HAZARD OF INSATIABLE GREED
(12:13-21)

In the parable of the Rich Fool, a man covets a larger share of the family inheritance and another man cherishes his possessions too much. The inheritance matter probably grows out of a practice in Jewish culture in which the eldest son inherits two portions of the estate and other sons inherit only one portion each. The son who approaches Jesus is evidently jealous of his older brother and asks Jesus to intercede on his behalf for a larger share. Jesus uses the request as an opportunity to warn about the insidious tendency to covetousness, resulting from an overemphasis on the value of possessions.

The Apostle Paul admonished the Colossians to "put to death what is earthly in you, . . . and covetousness which is idolatry" [Col. 3:5]). Olin Binkley in an ethics lecture at Southeastern Seminary defined covetousness as "an insatiable greed for more and more." This could be akin to drinking salt water: the more you drink, the thirstier you become.

Jesus reinforces his warning about the peril of covetousness with a parable about a man who puts his total confidence in material possessions (ample goods laid up) for his security and enjoyment of life. Jesus calls his value system foolish because material possessions have value only in the physical life and do not in themselves make one rich toward God.

TRUSTING PROVIDENCE OR BEING ANXIOUS
(12:22-31)

In a passage that parallels almost exactly a section from the Sermon on the Mount (Matt. 6:25-33), Jesus urges his hearers to keep material and spiritual matters in proper relation and balance. He in no sense indicates that things such as food and clothing are not important, only that they are of temporal and passing value while the worth of life involves so much more. When Jesus compares people to birds and flowers, he is not encouraging idleness. Birds and flowers are parts of the animal and plant kingdoms controlled by natural laws and involving instinct. Some birds migrate and all have to search for food produced by nature. Squirrels store nuts, while some animals feed on plants or other animals in the food chain. People have evolved to the capacity to plan, produce, and save. The admonition by Jesus is about living anxiously as though God has no providential role in our lives.

A phrase in verse 25 is made clearer by a bit of word study. The word translated "cubit" means "a forearm" and is used as a measure of length (about 18 inches). The word translated "span of life" means "stature" or "the appropriate height of a person at each stage of maturity."[5] The rhetorical question about what anxiety can or cannot do is about adding a measure of length (cubit), so consistency should lead to "stature" in translation (as in the KJV). But "length" also refers to "span of life," so "cubit" is also an appropriate figure to mean "span of life." Anxiety can neither help a person grow higher nor live longer.

In verse 29 the instruction is to "neither seek food and clothing nor to be of anxious mind." The two are not contradictory. The word translated "seek" means "to seek, to desire, to strive after." The action is described as ongoing, as in going on seeking, going on desiring, going on striving.[6] The admonition by Jesus is to not become so concerned about food and clothing as to become obsessed and anxious. This in no way suggests idleness as an irresponsible neglect of intelligent planning and use of ability in providing physical needs. After all, while the birds neither sow nor reap, they do have to find the food they and their young need. Material things (food, clothing, physical beauty), if they become dominating factors in life, reveal both a lack of trust in God and a failure to recognize the preeminence of spiritual values ("seek first the Kingdom of God").

TRUST AND WISE LIVING
(12:32-34)

Following his warning about anxious living, Jesus describes what he means by seeking first the kingdom of God. He starts by assuring his hearers that God is beneficent. Through his caring love he wants to bestow blessing on us in a relationship of harmonious fellowship. Our part in that covenant of fellowship is to live by trust in God, and to be caring and generous toward others as God is toward us.

To "sell and give" does not call us to divest ourselves of all material possessions and embrace a lifestyle of abject poverty. It is an instruction to keep material and spiritual values in proper balance and to be good stewards of our material possessions. Only as we embrace and practice values that have lasting worth do we develop treasures that will accompany us to heaven. If our treasures are only those that belong to physical life in a material world, we will leave them behind when physical death releases us to the spiritual world of eternity.

TRUE CHARACTER
(12:35-48)

In two combined parables Jesus teaches about the importance of faithfulness and readiness. He speaks first of a man returning home from a wedding feast and finding his servants faithfully serving and expectantly waiting for his return. In an unexpected turn of the story the master shows his appreciation by having the servants sit at the table while he serves them.

On a different topic Jesus speaks of how a man would guard his house if he knew a thief or some danger was coming. He warns his hearers to be alert and watchful "for the Son of man is coming at an hour you do not expect." The traditional interpretation of "the Son of man is coming . . ." is a reference to the Second Coming and Judgment, but it is equally applicable to "the moment of death and end of physical life," which can come at any unexpected moment for anyone. Jesus simply says, "Be ready."

Simon Peter responds with a question: Is the warning/admonition a teaching for the disciples, or is it a principle of life applicable to all people? Jesus goes on to explain that faithfulness to responsibility will bring reward. Sloven disregard for responsibility will result in penalty and loss.

LEARNING, CHOOSING, LIVING
(12:49-59)

In the remainder of Luke 12 the writer records three brief items that deal with realities of life we would be wise to take seriously.

In verses 49-53 Jesus speaks about what I describe as "the consequences of incarnation." He clearly indicates that the purpose of God in incarnation is not simply to fit in with the status quo and go peacefully along with what is already in place in human society and in religion. Jesus understands human nature so well, he declares that people will divide over him—even among members of families. It seems evident that God intended to give a clearer and different revelation about himself and about the meaning of religion than people have been able to grasp and practice.

...

One of the fundamental features of being human is the capacity and necessity to make choices. When people are confronted with differing choices in religion, as with the difference between Jewish legalism and the faith/grace religion Jesus revealed, some will choose one and some will choose the other. If religious convictions are deep-seated enough to be really meaningful in life, it is extremely difficult for people to accept any significant changes in them. Authentic conversion between no religious commitment, devotion to a legalistic religion, or acceptance of a faith-based religion will result in a radical altering of life, but it will also sometimes cause rifts of division even within families.

...

In verses 54-56 Jesus points out to the crowd how difficult people find it to distinguish between physical and spiritual realities. By observing weather movements and their consequences, people have learned what to expect as outcomes from different situations. But people have proven to be less discerning about the consequences, of value choices, habit formation, and human behavior.

Hebrew history through the Old Testament reflects how spokesmen for God warned the nation that high standards of loyalty to God would bring well-being to the nation but that disregard for such loyalty to God's leadership would bring ill consequences. And yet the Hebrews periodically drifted away into the ways of physical and spiritual decadence and suffered the consequences.

In verses 57-59 Jesus urges the people to learn to distinguish and pursue practices that will be genuinely beneficial. To seek resolution is wiser than to strive to prevail by conflict—a victory won at too great a cost. To win a battle but lose the war is folly.

THE NECESSITY OF REPENTANCE
(13:1-5)

Some Pharisees thought of themselves as so "righteous" that they did not need repentance (see Luke 5:31-32). In Luke 13:1-5, Jesus illustrates even more clearly that repentance must be a way of life for any who would be in harmony with God.

No historical reference seems to exist for the two disasters Jesus mentions. The mingling of the blood of Galileans with their sacrifices is surely a reference to Pilate's cruelty and contempt for the Jews and their religious practices. The kind of event described is most likely a slaughter of Jews while they are involved in slaughtering animals for their ritual sacrifices. Siloam is one of the sacred pools in the temple area of Jerusalem. The fall of a wall seems to refer to some type of accident, perhaps when workmen are building or repairing a part of the surrounding wall.

In both instances the question involves whether the tragedies are caused by the sinfulness of the victims. Jesus does not declare the victims sinless, but neither does he agree with the questioners that the tragedies are caused by the sinfulness of the victims. In his answer Jesus points out that all people are sinful and that repentance is the only hope any of them have to avoid the perishing consequences of sinfulness.

...

These brief verses reinforce the importance of authentic repentance in a sinful person's reconciliation with God. Repentance in contemporary life is often treated as nothing more than a sinful person is sorry for having committed a sinful act, but metanonte *means far more.* Metanoia *(repentance) means "to change the mind and reverse the direction of life." Sinfulness means that people are out of harmony with God and alienated from his fellowship.*

Because we humans must of necessity see life from inside ourselves, we have an ongoing inevitable tendency to become self-centered. Our sinfulness results in our often drifting into bad habits, making wrong choices, not trusting God fully, having rebellious attitudes, and following disobedient practices in our lives and relationship to God.

Authentic repentance means that we choose a way of life that includes seriously examining our values, prayerfully checking on our harmony with God, and regularly, as needed, making a reorientation of life—a change of attitude toward God, a choice to trust God instead of ignoring God, the embrace of new values to provide motivation and action in life. In other words, repentance means a radical reorientation, embracing a new way of life, as in, what Jesus meant when he said "You must be born again (from above)."

...

CASTING OUT OR KEEPING IN
(13:6-9)

Jesus describes the difference in the ways two men respond to the failure of a fig tree to bear fruit. He crafts a beautiful word picture of a significant difference between the judgmental tendencies of people and the reconciling outreach of God. The owner of the fig tree reacts in a way that is very characteristic of the way people often think about things or people over which they have decision-making authority.

The fig tree is not producing the fruit the owner wants, so he considers it useless and says, "Cut it down." The vinedresser, on the other hand, displays an attitude more in keeping with the way God values people. He asks for permission to give the tree another chance, with help that he can give, to see if the tree can become fruitful. If not, then he will cut it down. (This attitude toward people is shown in Luke 10:3-12 when Jesus sends the disciples to go out and witness, but if people refuse to heed their message they are to leave and go to other places.)

ANOTHER SABBATH CONTROVERSY
(13:10-17)

When Jesus performs a healing on the Sabbath, he draws criticism from the synagogue leader. According to the strict practice of Jews in regard to Sabbath-keeping, everything must be set aside to avoid any violation of the sanctity of the Sabbath. Jesus, in response, replies that meeting human need is more important than ritual details about Sabbath observance. He points out how the Jews readily make exceptions about the day of rest so as to care for their own interests. Luke concludes the story by describing this as another of the reasons why the Jewish religious leaders so oppose Jesus and the common people favor him.

KINGDOM INSIGHTS
(13:18-21)

The two comparisons in Luke 13 about the kingdom of God are recorded in collections of teaching by Jesus in Mark 4 and Matthew 13. Both describe how the influence of God's sovereign reign and love in a person's life may begin as small and simple as a seed sown in the ground or a bit of yeast mixed into a batch of dough. But the dynamic influence of God's Spirit working grace in someone's life can totally transform that person.

· · ·

The gospel comes into our life as a "word," that becomes an "idea" or an "awareness," that becomes a "conviction." We do not capture ideas; we are captured by ideas. Once an idea fixes itself in our mind we can no longer think as we did before. The Spirit of God uses gleams of light to call us upward to new understandings and new trust in God. We can deny it and refuse it, and shut ourselves out from the blessings of a life in harmony with God, but doing so will only leave us impoverished.

· · ·

WIDE AND NARROW "DOORS"
(13:22-30)

Jesus is on his way to Jerusalem the last time. The "narrow gate/wide road" saying (Matt. 7:13-14) offers the same "end-time" teaching as the parable here about who is admitted into the house. When someone asks Jesus, "Lord, will those who are saved be few?" he answers that those who are "ready," who are "reconciled," who are living in harmony with God will be the ones welcomed "into God's house" at the final day. All other claims will be denied. No other pretenses will count.

...

The teachings of Jesus are a warning to all people: do not count on God to work some miracle at death to make a person who has had no faith commitment come into harmony with God. People have demonstrated clearly all through human history that we can do religious rituals in abundance without their having any transforming influence in our lives. Jesus taught in many ways that only religion rooted in life-focused, trusting faith in God will make real the new birth from above that reconciles sinful persons to God and makes them "belong at the table in the kingdom."

...

JESUS REVEALS HIS INTENT
(13:31-35)

Some Pharisees warn Jesus to change direction and go away from Jerusalem, as Herod wants to kill him. Since the Pharisees are so opposed to Jesus, his teachings and his actions, it seems strange that they would warn him instead of helping Herod with his cruel plans. One has to wonder if their motivation is not (I think) simply to frighten Jesus enough so he will stay away from Jerusalem and stop troubling them. Jesus tells them to inform Herod that he will follow his chosen course to its end without regard to the tyrant's designs. The lament over Jerusalem is an acknowledgement by Jesus that people in power have no tolerance for voices that challenge their positions. His chicken and her brood example reflects the *agape* (caring kindness) nature of God that reaches out even to his enemies, but he will not force them if they reject his offer of love and forgiveness.

...

In the wilderness at the beginning of his ministry, Jesus chose not to join the advocates of "power over people" as the method he would use to do the reconciling work for which he had become incarnate. Since we are persons gifted with free will, force can be used to restrain the body, but not the spirit. For the soul of man, "Stone walls do not a prison make, nor iron bars a cage."

Jesus came to Jerusalem deliberately to challenge the powers, both religious and civil, and to let them kill him. But by his death he let them destroy their own pretense of victory. He lived beyond death, eternally victorious.

There is a legend that, after the Resurrection was noised abroad, Pilate's wife asked the centurion who had been in command at the Crucifixion, "And where do you think he is now?" The centurion is said to have answered, "Let loose in the world, Ma'am, where neither Jew nor Roman can ever hinder him again." Jesus chose to offer us love and grace to draw us to trust and transforming conversion instead to trying to "make us get in line" by power.

...

A HEALING ON THE SABBATH
(14:1-6)

Jesus heals a man on a Sabbath while he is a guest in the home of a Pharisee official. Other people present, including Pharisees and lawyers, are watching Jesus, as in what has become a common practice among Jewish leaders who are critical of much he is saying and doing.

As in a previous incident (see Luke 13:10-17), the issue at hand is about healing on the Sabbath. Jesus teaches and practices that helping people in need is more important than obeying a detail of ritual requirement that will forbid such a helpful action. He again points out to the critics that they rationalize bypassing ritual requirements when it is for their benefit and convenience (their ox or ass in need).

PRIORITIES, PRIDE, AND HUMILITY
(14:7-24)

Jesus uses the setting of a dinner to teach lessons about pride and humility. He first addresses the guests (14:7-11), then the host (vv. 12-14). Next he talks about people invited to a festal occasion (vv. 15-24).

To the guests he warns that anyone who seeks honor by taking a prominent seat at a dinner might be embarrassed and humiliated by having to move to a less prominent seat to make way for a more eminent guest. Jesus admonishes his hearers to take a lower seat and if the host moves him up, the recognition will be an honor. (The danger of egotism and self-promotion seems to be a widespread human failing.)

In his counsel to the host who has invited him (v. 1), Jesus expands on the sayings recorded in Matthew (5:46-47). Jesus points out the difference between equals swapping favors and doing a deed of genuine helpful service to others who cannot repay. His point is, if we help someone who cannot repay us, then the outcome will be in the nature of blessing, something different than a return favor by an equal.

In response to Jesus' teachings, one of the fellow guests comes forth with an adulation of praise: "Blessed is he who . . ." Jesus continues with an example to teach a lesson about priorities. He describes how people often fail to grasp the value of occasions they meet.

According to the parable of the great dinner, a host for a banquet invites guests whom he expects to value his invitation. When banquet time comes and all preparations are complete, he learns that his invited guests do not value his invitation enough to come. Other things are more important to them, or more interesting, than his proffered feast. He responds by sending his servants to find and invite people who will value the offer enough to attend the banquet. Jesus has the host declare that the opportunity will not come again.

The lesson in this parable is fittingly applied to the offer of love and grace by God to us sinful humans. It is deceptively easy and tempting for people when faced with difficult moral choices to react as Felix did when Paul preached about justice and judgment, "Go away for now, I'll call you at a more convenient time" (Acts 24:25).

DECISIONS OF DISCIPLESHIP
(14:25-33)

Jesus is very forthright with those considering discipleship. He says that those who would follow him must "hate" their families. A parallel passage in Matthew (10:37) uses the expression "love more" instead of "hate." Many interpreters believe that "love less" instead of "hate" is a better understanding of this passage in Luke's tradition. This seems to be an acceptable position. While both *miseo* (Greek) and *SaNeA* (Hebrew) do have "to hate" as their basic meaning, in a modified form they are also used to refer to "relative esteem"—to love more or less.[8]

Jesus clearly says that divine/human relationships and divine/spiritual values must take precedence over human/human relationships and human/physical values. God must be first priority, and spiritual values must be primary if we are to live in harmony with God and be followers of Jesus.

Jesus also tells his would-be followers to take up their cross, consider carefully the cost of discipleship, and give up their possessions. All the choices and decisions we make have consequences involved in the follow-up actions. Following Jesus calls for deep and serious commitments, and Jesus never promises us it will be easy.

...

The statement about taking up and bearing one's cross is troublesome for me. Romans dominated the culture in which Jesus and his followers lived, and they used crucifixion as the most cruel and debasing form of execution. Only after Jesus was crucified and transformed the cross into a symbol of love for people and devotion to righteousness would it have been possible for anyone to consider "taking up a cross" to be a call to faithful dedication (see comments on Luke 9:23.)

The statement about "renouncing all that he has" also raises questions. The word in the text is a form of apotasso, *whose basic meaning is "to set apart, say farewell to, take leave of, renounce." Did Jesus teach that we are required to abandon all family and rid ourselves of all possessions in order to follow him?*

I have to believe that Jesus calls on us to establish for ourselves relative values for people and things to keep our priorities in order. As the phrase in Matthew 6:33 seems

57

*to mean, "Seek first his (God's) kingdom, and all these things (food, clothing, etc.)
shall be yours as well (i.e. you will have them, you will have control over them, and
you will be able to keep them in proper relative value)."*

...

"UNSALTY" SALT
(14:34-35)

On the subject of genuine discipleship, we find a parallel passage in the Sermon on the
Mount (Matt. 5:13). Salt has no value apart from its authentic quality of saltiness. If it is
not salty, it is not salt. Jesus is apparently referring to salt that is so fully saturated into other
materials that it has no salty quality, and no use as salt. This idea is similar to the reference
in the parable of the sower to the seed that falls among thorns and bears no fruit because it
is completely choked out. These words by Jesus follow appropriately the previous passage.
Anyone who is not freely willing to embrace and live by the truths and values Jesus reveals
by his life and teachings cannot be his follower.

...

*For sinful people, a transforming conversion of life by repentance and faith, with grace
and forgiveness by God, is essential to become a follower of Jesus. The presence of the
Holy Spirit guiding and helping every day is essential to faithful following of Jesus.
Being a Christian is a distinctively transformed (salty) life. It must be real or it has
no reality.*

...

LOST AND FOUND
(15:1-2)

Luke 15 seems to be a group of teachings by Jesus on a common or similar theme but shared
at different times and places. (This feature seems to be true also of the Sermon on the Mount
in Matthew 5–7 and the group of kingdom parables in Matthew 13.) The common theme is
the redeeming care God has for persons who are alienated from him by their sinfulness, and
the gracious purpose of God to restore them to reconciled fellowship with himself.

In the opening verses of Luke 15 the scribes and Pharisees are criticizing Jesus for
associating with "sinners." To these Jewish religious leaders, being sinful means not abiding
by all the ritual requirements that have developed through more than a thousand years of
Hebrew cultural development and religious practices. According to them, violation of any
washing, cleansing, or sacrificial practice puts a person outside the favor of God and any
acceptability for association. In three parables Jesus emphasizes for the religious leaders the
reconciling purpose of God.

The "lost and found" parables demonstrate what Paul will later write about God's purpose in the incarnation of Jesus, ". . . in Christ God was reconciling the world unto himself, not counting their trespasses against them . . ." (2 Cor. 5:19). Logizomai means to take into account, to consider a person or thing of worth or not, an event as important or unimportant.

THE LOST SHEEP
(15:3-7)

In the first parable a sheep has become "lost" or separated from the flock. The parable does not describe how this happens, whether by accidentally getting trapped in brambles, by falling down a cliff, or by simply wandering away as it grazes. The point of the parable is about the action of the shepherd who cares so much for his sheep that he goes to find it, rescue it, and bring it back into the fold with his flock. There is no hint that the shepherd does not value each of the other sheep equally as much, but the sheep that needs rescuing is the one that needs his action. And rescue (repentance and reconciliation) is a source of joy.

A MISPLACED COIN
(15:8-10)

In the second parable a coin has become misplaced. A coin is a thing, so obviously it has not become "lost" by any action of the coin but by the action of its owner. The point of the parable is that the woman's concern for the coin is so great, she is willing to do what is necessary to search for and find it. This parable is not about how the coin becomes lost, but about the value the woman places on the coin and her willingness to act to recover it.

The parable does not instruct us about how sinners become lost, for it is certainly not by any action of God that sinners have become alienated from him. The parable is about the great love that God has for sinners, the value he places on everyone, and the recovering action he has taken by incarnation to reconcile sinners unto himself.

THE PRODIGAL SON
(15:11-32)

The most familiar—and favorite—of the three parables is the one we refer to as the prodigal son. Most interpreters treat this parable as revealing the caring and forgiving character of God, but it also instructs us about other matters. The relationship between the brothers reflects the "second son syndrome."

In the early twentieth century, clinical psychologists described features characteristic of second sons or middle children that develop as a result of the attitudes and actions of adults who have already experienced parenthood with a first child. The second child is not so exciting, not so many pictures are taken of her, and she may well be left feeling neglected in a much busier household. The characteristics are also influenced by experiences between siblings, since the older has learned to do almost everything ahead of the younger, and the younger never seems to be able to "catch up." There was a distinct feature in Hebrew culture that reflects this family dynamic.

The first son inherited clan headship and a double portion of the family estate. This inheritance was a point of conflict in the biblical story where Rebekah and Jacob schemed to secure the "first son" privilege for Jacob, instead of Isaac's intention to bestow the "clan blessing" on Esau (Gen. 25:27–27:38). This same family dynamic is reflected in British nobility of the nineteenth century.

This same family dynamic is reflected in British nobility of the nineteenth century in which the first son inherited the noble title and the central part of the estate. A commission in the royal navy was secured for the second son. If there was a third son, an appointment in the clergy was sought for him.[9]

So, it does not seem strange that the younger son in the parable is restless and wants to get out of the family situation and from under the shadow of his "obedient" and "favored" brother. His trying his own wings reflects the consequences of his immature and rebellious choices.

Note also the characteristics of the older brother. He obviously understands and accepts his privileged position within the family. He stays at home, obeys his father, and is careful not to do anything that will jeopardize his privileged position in the family or diminish the value of the inheritance coming to him. But when his prodigal brother returns, he pouts and whines about the waste of resources for a feast and his feeling that he has not been properly recognized with allowances for parties he obviously had expected in the past.

The father's agreement to let the younger son have the inheritance resources coming to him reflects the pattern of responsibility and opportunity God has bestowed on human persons when God causes us to develop with the gift of freedom of choice and the capacity of free will to choose a system of values and a course of life to follow. Note that the father does not go to find his wayward son and "bring him home," as the shepherd in the first of these parables goes to find and bring home his absent sheep. (The lost sheep does not have the capacity nor responsibility to make moral choices.) The prodigal son has to change his mind (repent) and want to be a part of the father's family before he will choose to come home.

This parable reflects the experience of repentance and the choice to return by the wayward son. The father has obviously been longing, hoping, and waiting for the son to come home. When he sees his son coming, he gladly runs to welcome him and compassionately forgive the wayward choices he has made. Welcoming him home is a joyful celebration.

The father's interchange with the older son reflects the same truth expressed in the ending of the two earlier parables: the repentance and reconciliation of alienated sinful people is a reason for joy and celebration to God. The father assures his older son that the return of the prodigal does not change nor diminish their relationship. ("Son, you are always with me and all that is mine is yours," v. 31). The return of the younger brother does not take anything away from the older brother, but the prodigal's return is a reason for celebration because he is a valued part of the family: "he was lost and is found."

Jesus does not finish the story, so we are left with questions: Does the younger son turn out to be a decent and responsible guy in the long run? Does the older brother get over his self-centered concerns and accept his brother into the family again?

...

The character of God is clearly revealed in the attitudes and actions of the father in the parable. God has so much regard for us as humans, he will not violate our personhood. He gives us freedom of choice and will not take it away from us. He will let us be "prodigal" if we choose. He will let us be "pouty and self-centered" if we choose. But he loves us unconditionally, just as we are, right here and now; and he always waits, hopes, reaches out, and pleads with us to "come home into his family" because he wants to have us live in harmony and fellowship with him more than anything else. There is joy in heaven whenever one sinner repents.

...

"WORLD SMART" OR "SPIRITUAL SMART"?
(16:1-9)

The story about the dishonest steward is not called a parable, but it fits the pattern of parables in that it has a central teaching. The steward is a scheming rascal. His employer becomes aware that he is either incompetent or a thief and therefore calls him to account. The steward in turn instructs his employer's debtors to reduce the amounts they owe by a fifth to a half. His motivation appears to be to get them indebted to him in hope of some later return of favors, or maybe to put them in a position to be blackmailed. His employer commends him for acting practically in his situation (I would call it acting greedily dishonest).

The last statement in verse 8 and all of verse 9 reveal the heart of the meaning of this passage: people make their choices in light of their values. Those who value material things and physical pleasures are often shrewder in plans or manipulations to secure for themselves the things they want than the "sons of light" (those who value and seek to practice and enhance honesty, fairness, helpfulness, generosity, etc.).

...

What Jesus taught and practiced clearly reveals there are needs and values that belong to the physical and sensate part of our lives that are temporal and passing, on one hand, and the values and actions that reside in the spiritual realm and determine the quality of our character, the kind of people we are, and are of eternally meaningful consequences. Jesus made telling comments about which of these sets of values prove to be most attractive and compelling in many people's lives.

Physical needs are of vital concern as long as we are physically alive. Pleasant experiences are more desirable than unpleasant ones, and so we are readily inclined to seek the pleasant ones. Our challenge in life is to assess carefully and to choose both the physical and spiritual values that enable us to be persons of faithfulness instead of faithlessness, honesty instead of dishonesty, kindness instead of cruelty; for only when our lives are so characterized can we live in harmony and fellowship with God. There is a dire warning in the words about making friends with unrighteous values and ways of life. There is something ominous about "eternal habitations."

...

INTEGRITY

(16:10-13)

Jesus continues his teaching with an emphasis on integrity. His examples reflect that integrity is a matter of character and not volume of ownership. An honest person is honest whether an amount involved is a few dollars or a few thousand, whether the money belongs to him or to another. Integrity and honesty come from the values a person chooses to consider most important. The example Jesus uses of God and mammon (money) refers to spiritual and eternal values in life in contrast to material and temporal values. Jesus does not teach that material concerns are unimportant; after all, he heals sick bodies and feeds hungry people.

...

The scriptures reveal that humans have a physical life that is material and mortal, but we also have a spiritual dimension (a soul) that bears the image of God and is immortal. Our choice of values will cause us to prioritize one over the other and to give to each the relative concern we choose to believe its value merits. To discern the relative importance of them and to choose the most important over the less important determines whether we serve God or mammon.

...

WHAT WE BELIEVE AND TRUST
(16:14-18)

The harsh charge that Pharisees are lovers of money seems valid from their attitude toward Jesus. They scoff at Jesus and dispute everything he says and does. He replies that they can set forth their teachings and maintain their status as religious leaders in the society, but God knows their true character. This declaration is another of the many indications in the Gospels that Jesus in his incarnation is revealing a character of God and a meaning and purpose for religion that is radically different from the beliefs about God and the practices of religion that have developed and are being practiced in the Judaism that prevailed before Jesus.

The statement "what is exalted among men is an abomination in the sight of God" needs comment. The words for "exalt" (*upsalon*) and "abominate" (*bdelugma*) stand side by side in the text and emphasize their contrast.[10] *Upsalon* denotes height and is used here to describe the height of a mountain, the eminence of a person, or the value of a treasure. The basic meaning of *bdelugma* is offensive or repulsive, something that stinks, something that causes a person to turn away, to hate, to detest. Since the subject here has to do with serving "God or mammon," the statement refers to what people choose to value and how God responds to those choices. It seems the meanings are relative and not absolute because they differ with different people and about things in our lives and our relationships with God.

The degree to which we "exalt" material things in relative comparison to the value we give to our spiritual lives in relation to God leads to the way God responds to our choices and our lives in return. And it is abominable to God when "mammon" is the most highly prized value in our lives, not because material values are "repulsive" to God, but because too much "love of money" becomes idolatry to us and keeps us from a devoted relationship of trust and harmony with him.

The prologue to the Fourth Gospel includes this definitive statement, "The law was given through Moses; grace and truth came through Jesus Christ" (John 1:17). The statement that "The law and the prophets were until John" (Luke 16:16) indicates that John the Baptist was considered to be the transitional person who represented a change from a religion of law and sacrifice to a religion of grace and reconciliation. Remember, John required persons to "bear fruits that befit repentance" (Luke 3:8) as a witness to changed life as a reason for baptism.

The summary statement that "everyone enters it violently" (RSV) has an alternate KJV translation, "presseth into it." This is preferable. The basic idea in the Greek word *bia* is impetus, or force—as in using violent force or in describing the driving impetus behind actions that are not violent in nature.[11] The idea of "urgent striving" seems to fit what we find in examples of people crowding around Jesus to get to him for healing, seeking to see wonderworks, trying to hear his teaching. His popularity with the masses indicates that the crowds want to be a part of what is going on, and that desire is the urgency described here.

The reference to the enduring validity of the law in verse 17 must certainly be to the faithfulness to covenant and the obedience in relationship with God that were the foundation of Israel's religion from Abraham and Moses to Jesus. Every "dot of the law" surely is not a reference to every detail of ritual about washings, cleansings, sacrifices, and Sabbath conduct. In his teachings and practice Jesus affirms that these are not the essence of trust and faithfulness in relationship to God.

In his statement of the two great commandments (Matt. 22:34-40) Jesus says that all of the law "depends on" (*kremannumi* = to hang, i.e. to draw meaning from)[12] what it means to love God and one's neighbor and oneself. Love here is agape (to care about), not phileo (to like as a friend). So, all of the "practices" of the law draw their meaning from what enhances the quality of life and relationships with God, with one's neighbor, and with oneself. If a ritual or religious practice enhances love of God and neighbor, follow it. If not, Jesus "said" to let it go and let the Spirit lead you into a way of life that does.

Verse 18 that equates divorce and remarriage with adultery has been interpreted by much of traditional Christianity and applied literally to mean physical and permanently ongoing sexual unfaithfulness. We ought not forget the obvious allegorical example in the book of Hosea. The physical adultery of Gomer is described in that allegory to represent Israel's unfaithfulness to the covenant. The action of Hosea to buy her back out of slavery and woo her back to a faithful relationship with him represents the forgiving love and reconciling work of God toward Israel.

· · ·

When marriage is believed to be, and is entered into, as fundamentally a covenant between two people who commit themselves to a shared lifetime of "richer or poorer, sickness and health," then any time that relationship breaks apart, one or both of the partners has not lived up to what they promised, to the covenant they made. Violation of the covenant can result from cruelty (physical or mental) by one against the other, by failure to share in the responsibilities of family, by simple desertion, as surely as by an unfaithful sexual affair. A covenant relationship can survive only through faithful commitment (physically, devotedly, responsibly, morally, truthfully, with integrity) by both persons. No other kind of marriage can genuinely survive. And relationships can die, just as people can.

· · ·

GREAT GULFS
(16:19-31)

The story about a rich man and a beggar has been widely debated with disagreement about its meaning. It is exclusive with Luke and reflects the characteristic of Luke's Gospel that emphasizes Jesus' concern for the poor and outcast of human society.

Note the difference in traditions behind the Gospel writers as recorded in the Beatitudes when speaking of the poor: "Blessed are you poor" (Luke 6:20) vs. "Blessed are the poor in spirit" (Matt. 5:3).

Note also Jesus' warning about the danger of riches: "Woe to you that are rich, for you have received your consolation" (Luke 6:24). In other scriptures he speaks of the effect of wealth on the character of a person (see Matt. 19:24, Mark 10:25, and Luke 18:25).

The story makes no distinction between the two men except that one is rich and the other is poor. Nothing about their character or behavior is recorded. After they die the poor man is in beatitude and the rich man is in anguish. This reversal of conditions is due to their situations in life before death (v. 25)

We can surmise that the rich man of the story has become self-centered and obsessed with his wealth because of his disregard and lack of concern for the poor beggar. The story and its conclusion do not teach this about him, however. Neither does it teach that the poor man is a person of good character and an upright lifestyle, and that he is an innocent victim of unfortunate circumstances. The poor man may be greedy and cruel just as the rich man may be proud and pompous. The rich man may also be humble, generous, and kind. Character is not determined by the amount of a person's possessions.

...

The difficulty of understanding this story, as with the earlier story about a dishonest, manipulating employee being commended (16:1-9), raises a question about the background of the tradition Luke received as he searched for stories about the life and teachings of Jesus (see Luke 1:2-3). Did the Christians in Asia Minor take stories they had heard about Jesus and through decades of retelling them shorten, expand, or refocus them?

...

The concluding verses of Luke 16 contain a warning that ought not be ignored. When people have received a proclamation, whether it be from Moses and the prophets or of the Christian gospel, and have chosen to believe it is not a trustworthy guide for values and practices in life, they will not likely believe differently even if someone "should rise from the dead."

...

Jesus died and rose two thousand years ago, but millions still pay no heed to what he taught and how he lived. Freedom of choice is an awesomely great blessing by the design and gift of God, but it also places an equally great responsibility on every one of us as we choose and chart a path through life by free will. Hebrews 12:2 has a wise and inspired admonition, ". . . looking unto Jesus, the pioneer and perfecter of our faith."

...

EXAMPLE AND INFLUENCE

(17:1-6)

Luke continues his inclusion of teachings that give every indication of being a collection of traditions without time or location indicated. Jesus begins this discussion with a forthright comment that "temptations . . . are sure to come." Both good and bad influences will be an ongoing part of everyday life. The example of our lives will be either good or bad influence on others, especially children. How we respond to the examples and influences around us will be a part of determining the kind of people we become. Jesus goes on to say that we are individually responsible for the effect our influence has on other people and for how we respond to the effect of influence by others on us.

...

When we live in community among others instead of in isolation, we influence others just as they influence us. Having authentic concern for each other is a vital part of harmonious and general well-being in community. A part of living in relationship with others inevitably means that disagreements and conflicts will occur, sometimes intentionally and sometimes unintentionally. Forgiveness is necessary if such inter-personal problems are to be corrected without lasting hurt to one or both parties.

...

Jesus declares that people who want to follow him will actively seek to resolve their interpersonal problems: "rebuke him" (make sure the other person is aware of the problem; and if that leads to repentance and reconciliation, the problem is over and done with). Jesus encourages his followers to make their enemies their friends and to be forgivers, even to unlimited times.

Jesus is not suggesting the "easy way," for forgiveness is a difficult response to harsh wrongs that sometimes occur. In response the apostles ask, "Increase our faith." It takes a lot of faith in the rightness of forgiving initiative to seek to reduce the cruelty and hurt in human relations instead of seeking revengeful justice that increases such hurt. Jesus reinforces his emphasis on the powerful influence of faith by declaring that faith is the key to being able to forgive, just as faith is the key to living in the kingdom of God (see Rom. 5:1-2).

...

Our understanding of the importance of being forgiving is surely informed by the importance that God's forgiveness of our sinfulness has on his reconciling us into a harmony of relationship. Reconciliation of sinful people has always been more important to God than requiring punishment or recompense for sinfulness (see 2 Cor. 5:19). God is an "upfront" forgiver, a "make the first move" reconciler, and Jesus calls on his followers to "have faith in God" and follow that example.

Jesus does not speak about what we should do if an injuring or offending person shows no care and asks no forgiveness. Many of the hurts that come to us come from people with whom we have no personal or communal relationship. And there are sometimes people who within a community refuse to believe they have done anything wrong, even though others feel deep hurt. So where does that leave us?

We often hear it said that you cannot forgive unless you forget. That is a tragic error: forgiveness and forgetting are two different things. Forgiveness has to do with a damaged relationship, not an intellectual memory. Forgiveness means that a healed relationship is more important to an injured person than what the injuring person has done. Now it surely helps when an injurer recognizes that he/she has caused hurt, cares about it, and with real regret asks forgiveness. Forgiving means the relationship is healed, but neither is likely to actually "forget" it. And, what if the offender just doesn't care about the relationship? Where does that leave a person who has been "sinned against"?

I am convinced that being a forgiving person is far more important, more liberating, and more Christlike than holding grudges and getting even. Surely Jesus would have us be the kind of person who wants to forgive and heal a relationship or is willing to forgive and desire a good relationship. Still, it takes a lot of faith—the kind that transforms life and gives strength to life—to forgive as God forgives.

...

OBEDIENCE, FAITH, AND GRATITUDE
(17:7-19)

Several times in Luke (chs. 12, 17, 22), Jesus teaches that true greatness reflects itself by serving and benefitting others, not by self-enhancement. Luke 17 emphasizes an attitude of obedient fulfillment of responsibility: "We have only done what was our duty."

The statement is a continuation of the travel narrative section as Jesus is moving toward Jerusalem (see 9:51). From a geographical point of view, it seems that the references are reversed here. Galilee is north of Samaria, and Jerusalem is to the south. The direction of travel would normally be from Galilee through Samaria to Jerusalem.

As Jesus enters a village, ten lepers approach him. According to customary requirements, the lepers live in isolation away from contact with any other people, even family, because the disease is thought to be contagious and a cause for ritual uncleanness. The lepers ask for mercy, entreating Jesus for help and healing. Jesus instructs them to go and show themselves to the priests. This is not a promise that the priests can cure them but for the priests to certify that they are healed. This certification is required before they can return to their homes and to normal living in their community. Their willingness to go to the priests should give evidence of their faith that Jesus has healed them; if they are not healed, a visit to the priest will be of no consequence.

One of the lepers, when he becomes aware that he has been healed, comes back and thanks Jesus. In return, Jesus makes a telling response in the question, "Where are the nine?" Only one expresses gratitude, and he is a Samaritan. This is another evidence of Luke's emphasis on the universal focus of Jesus and the inclusion of all people in the love and care of God.

The concluding comment, "Your faith has made you well," reflects the importance of faith in our relationship to God and in the totality of our lives. What we have faith in is what we trust, and what we trust is what we live by. And, whether we are grateful or not will reflect the quality of our character ("a tree is known by the fruit it bears").

THE KINGDOM OF GOD

(17:20-37)

The remainder of Luke 17 is about Hebrew beliefs concerning "end times." Different ideas are set forth in the texts of scripture about end times: the coming of the kingdom of God, the day of judgment, the end of the world, the Day of the Lord, the coming of the Son of Man. Different kinds of "signs" are believed to be indications and warnings that the "end" is about to happen.

During the centuries after the Hebrew nation(s) were destroyed by the military dominance of great empires (Assyria, Babylon, Persia, Greece, and Rome) there arose among the Jews a messianic hope that God would raise up a new son of David, anointed with divine leadership, guidance, and ability, who would be thus enabled to defeat the hated adversaries and make Jerusalem the center of an eternal messianic Hebrew Kingdom of God. They believed the "Kingdom" would be a physical, geographical realm, centered in the city of Jerusalem.

Throughout the Gospels there are recorded times when Jesus meets expressions of these messianic hopes, such as when he does supernatural things and people want to make him king, hoping he is that dreamed-of and hoped-for Messiah. Jesus tries time and again to help them "unlearn" that mistaken idea about his mission and to help them "learn" that he is not that kind of Messiah—that his incarnate mission is a different kind of mission.

The Pharisees ask Jesus when the coming of the kingdom of God will be. Jesus tells them it will not be the kind of event they are expecting; that the kingdom of God is not coming with "signs to be observed" or as a physical kingdom. Nor will they find it by looking "here" or "there." Where, then, is the kingdom of God to be found?

Here translations differ: "within you" (KJV, NIV), "in the midst of you" (RSV), "among you" (*The Message*). The word in the text is *entos,* the adverbial form of the preposition *en* (in), answering the question of where.[13] There is further insight in the word translated "you." The word *humon* is a genitive plural, a possessive plural pronoun, meaning "within your," but it has no definition of "your what."[14]

There is widespread agreement that the kingdom of God as Jesus refers to it is a spiritual realm. Two interpretations of this verse have been widely used. Since Jesus is the Son of God incarnate, his presence represents the sovereign rule of God in the universe. So, since Jesus is present with them, the "Kingdom" is "among them" or "in the midst of them." This interpretation is reflected in the RSV and *Message* translations. The question in the text, however, is about where the kingdom is to be found, where the sovereign will of God is in effect. The better translation/interpretation of the adverb *entos* seems to be "within you(r)" (KJV, NIV), to which I would add from the context "within your kind of people."

...

I believe the "Kingdom" refers to the devoted acceptance of and obedience to the sovereign will of God in the hearts, spirits, souls, and lives of people who trust in God, embrace with faith God's lordship in their lives, and strive to live in obedience to God's guidance and commands. This understanding certainly reflects the distinction Jesus reveals between those who are reconciled to God and those who are alienated from God. (It is beautifully described about the "reconciled" in 1 Peter 2:9, "You are a chosen race, a royal priesthood, a holy nation, God's own people.")

Everyone will have to answer for themselves whether they believe "Kingdom" means a place—which is a physical, geographic concept—or a spiritual realm—where the sovereign will of God who is Eternal Spirit is embraced, trusted, and obeyed. The latter, I believe, is the "Kingdom" Jesus revealed.

...

In the remaining verses of Luke 17, Jesus uses graphic images from Jewish messianic eschatology to describe situations from ancient Jewish history and then to note the differences that actual "end of times" will bring. The images describe that in all generations—past, present, and future—through our physical lives we live among a world of people who through the gift of moral choice and free will choose either to follow the "way that leads to life" (Matt. 7:14) or to go the "way of the world." The two ways end in radically different ways. At the "end" of physical life everyone will find themselves in the consequences of the choices they have made, the way they have lived, and the persons they have become. In the "end" each of us will experience the "ultimate" outcome of the "kingdom" to which we belong.

PERSEVERING AT PRAYER
(18:1-8)

In a parable Jesus teaches about the practice of prayer, the importance of perseverance, and the role of faith. The parable is about a judge who has no regard for anything except his role as a judge and his comfort at doing that work. The widow perseveres in her pleas. The judge grows tired of her continual pleading and rules in her favor just to keep her from bothering him.

Jesus makes a contrast between God and the judge. If a judge who cares not a whit about us can be badgered into giving us something by perseverance, then surely God who cares so deeply for us will hear our prayers in all circumstances of life and answer with his gracious help to us, to endure injustice, to gain relief, to find peace, to experience beatitude. So, keep on praying. We cannot waste a prayer.

We can draw another helpful lesson from this parable. Since God is surely "on our side" when we are unjustly injured by an adversary, God also cares about us when we have chosen ways of life that are harmful to our well-being, physical as well as spiritual. So, if we will be as concerned about the effects of our chosen actions on our lives as we are about the treatment of others toward us, then persevering prayer for God's help with insight, encouragement, guidance, and help is a fitting way for us to express our trust in God.

The passage ends with a summary question, "Will the people of God persevere in faith?" People will only seek what they believe is worth seeking. People will make prayer a vital part of their ongoing lives only if they trust in God and believe he cares enough to hear and respond with love and grace.

WHAT COUNTS WITH GOD
(18:9-14)

Jesus uses a comparison of a Pharisee (one of the "in crowd") and a tax collector (one of the "out crowd") to teach a lesson about egotism and self-awareness. Context is important.

The Pharisees are considered to be the exemplary followers of every detail of Mosaic rituals, and they think of themselves as more righteous than anyone—Gentile or Jew—who is not equally devoted to the Torah. However, they seem to be blind to the sinfulness of arrogant pride. The tax collectors are Jews who work as contract revenue agents for the Roman government, and thus are considered by "faithful" Jews to be traitors to their Jewish heritage.

In the temple the Pharisee demonstrates freely his self-righteousness and his judgmental contempt for the tax collector. The tax collector reflects his self-awareness that he is sinful. The Pharisee boasts in his prayer and apparently expects to be commended by God. The tax collector confesses his sinfulness and prays for mercy. Jesus comments that self-righteous egotism doesn't get God's commendation, but humble searching for forgiveness and help in upright living does.

JESUS AND LITTLE CHILDREN
(18:15-19)

In ancient times children and women were not as highly valued in the patriarchal culture of the biblical centuries as adult men. The disciples have not embraced the "spirit of Jesus" in regarding all persons as valuable. They consider children bothersome distractions and try to shoo them away. Jesus corrects the disciples, expresses his welcome for the children, and teaches a lesson on the transforming influence of childlikeness.

What are the characteristics of childlikeness that help to fit us for belonging in the kingdom of God? Three are primary:

1. Candor—which causes children to be easily and openly honest
2. Curiosity—which causes children to be exploring, inquisitive, examining, and learning
3. Trustfulness—which causes children to be believing, accepting, expecting, hoping, and not given to suspicion

Such qualities of character help us to be open to God, to trust his grace, to be assured about his caring love, and to base our hope on his promises and his help.

WHERE OUR TREASURE IS
(18:18-30)

A wealthy man asks Jesus what he must do to inherit eternal life. He seems to expect praise from Jesus by his first flattering address, "Good Teacher." He evidently considers himself already in a very commendable position, for he declares that he has always been a keeper of the commandments. (Note that the commandments Jesus names are about behavior in relation to other people, not the first commandments in the Ten about relationship to God.)

Jesus affirms that such conduct is admirable, and then he exposes the true nature of the man's values by an admonition about his wealth: Stop making it the most important thing in your life. Free yourself from its dominance by selling it and giving some, or all of it, to the poor. Jesus tells the rich man to sell "all, as much as you have."

It appears to push the meaning when translators make the word *diados* mean "give it all away and become a pauper." (The root meaning of *diadidomi* is "to deliver from hand to hand, distribute, divide," which could as readily mean "to share" as "to give it all away.")[15] Jesus is calling on the man to stop trusting in riches, to embrace and live by values that are more excellent and permanent by following Jesus. The man is not willing to make this choice, however, so he goes away sad. The encounter has not turned out in the approving praise and status-enhancing way he had hoped and anticipated.

Jesus comments about how hard it is for many people to value spiritual well-being over material things. He focuses his comment on wealthy people, but any observation of human behavior reveals that the problem of choosing relative values is just as difficult for people in all levels of social and economic situations. The exaggerated contrast of a camel passing through the eye of a needle is meant by Jesus to create an image of something that is impossible for a human to do. His image receives exactly the reaction he expects: "That's impossible!" The summary statement by Jesus, "What is impossible with men is possible with God," (v. 27) declares the truth that only by faith in God is there grace and help to give hope to any of us.

Simon Peter's obvious question on behalf of the disciples, behind his comment, "We have left all (*panta*—everything)[16] to follow you," implies what is recorded as an explicit question in Matthew (19:27): "What then shall we have?" Jesus assures them that when anyone chooses the ways of the kingdom of God, the outcome will be abundant spiritual blessing.

The disciples seem to be struggling to sort things out as they follow Jesus. Just before the beginning of Passion Week they argue about who is greatest (Luke 9:46), and the mother of James and John asks Jesus for special honor for her sons in the "coming kingdom" (Matt. 20:20-21). Long-held hopes for an earthly messianic kingdom, with all the exalted privileges included, are deeply seated in the expectations of Jews. The disciples of Jesus are as human in their anticipations as any of their fellow Jews.

PREPARING THE DISCIPLES
(18:31-34)

As part of the "going up to Jerusalem" narrative, Luke records another of the statements by Jesus that he will be delivered to Gentiles and killed but then will rise. There are eight passages (almost identical) in the Synoptic Gospels that record the statement by Jesus about his approaching death in Jerusalem (Matt. 16:21, 17:22-23, 20:17-19; Mark 8:31, 9:31, 10:32-34; Luke 9:22, 18:32-33). The common parts of the statement are:

- rejection by Jewish religious authorities
- deliverance to Gentiles
- killed
- rise after three days

In none of these recorded statements does Jesus even imply that his death will be an atoning sacrifice to cleanse human sin guilt. This understanding of the meaning of the death of Jesus seems to have arisen among the early Christians as a perfect and adequate fulfillment of the ritual blood sacrifice of atonement that was central to Judaism.

The disciples respond to Jesus with confusion and disbelief, reflecting their Jewish heritage. Jesus does not teach like the rabbis who quote Moses and the prophets for authority. Jesus teaches on his own authority: "I say unto you." By teaching and by practice, he reveals that rituals such as cleansing by washing, and observing details about the Sabbath, are less important than meeting human needs and living upright moral lives. But his statements about his approaching death are the most difficult of all for his followers to understand. The Jewish messianic hope of the past six centuries has been that the Messiah would not be subject to death.[17] As the disciples are becoming able to believe that Jesus is the hoped-for Messiah, they simply cannot comprehend the idea that he can be killed. Again, the disciples have to "unlearn" from their Jewish heritage before they can embrace the fullness of the revelation made by Jesus in his incarnation.

COMPASSION AND ACTION
(18:35-43)

The disciples are near Jericho and approaching Jerusalem, just a dozen miles away going from the Jordan River valley up the eastern slope of the Judean mountains. As has happened many times before, Jesus meets a case of human need: a blind beggar sitting by the roadside. On learning that Jesus is passing by, he calls out for mercy and help. Ignoring rebukes, he keeps calling out. Jesus grants his request to receive sight, and he and the amazed crowd give praise to God.

ZACCHAEUS, THE NEW MAN
(19:1-10)

The familiar story about Zacchaeus and the sycamore tree is recorded only in Luke, which indicates it is a part of the "L" material, items that Luke received in the traditions he was able to learn as he "followed all things closely" (1:3) after he became a Christian.

Jesus and his followers are in Jericho, on their way to Jerusalem. Zacchaeus, a tax collector, is not the most highly respected man in town. He evidently has heard about Jesus, that he is known for associating with folks like himself. When he learns that Jesus is coming through town, his interest is sparked and he wants to see him. He has a problem, though: he is small of stature. So, he climbs a tree. Then the story takes an unexpected turn. Instead of passing on as everyone expects him to do, Jesus stops and looks up at Zacchaeus and invites himself to go with Zacchaeus to his house. Of course, the haughty Jewish leaders who constantly stalk Jesus do their usual criticizing, but Zacchaeus welcomes Jesus.

Now Zacchaeus is rich; evidently, he has been doing what is common among the Jewish tax collectors who are contractors for the Roman government: defrauding the people and collecting too much in taxes. Being in the presence of Jesus apparently stirs a guilty conscience, so Zacchaeus declares: "Half of my goods I give to the poor," and anything I collected by fraud "I restore fourfold." Jesus declares that "Salvation has come to this house, since he is also a son of Abraham." (This is an affirmation of the heritage of Abraham as a "man of faith.") Jesus sees in Zacchaeus such a repentant change in his values of life that "his faith" has brought him into harmony with God. This is not an example of "salvation by good works," but a witness that faith involves repentance that results in conversion and a new life, both in relationship with God and in conduct of life.

FAITHFULNESS AND STEWARDSHIP
(19:11-27)

In a parable about trust, responsibility, and consequences Luke describes the setting as being near Jerusalem. The people have just been present at the Zacchaeus event. There is excited anticipation and hope that the messianic kingdom of God will appear and be established—that Jesus just might be the promised Messiah. This parable is very similar to the parable of the talents in Matthew (25:14-30), but there are variances in the number of servants and the amounts of money.

In Luke 19 a nobleman has enough trust in ten of his servants to leave with them amounts to invest while he is away. He gives each one pound. (The translation is confusing, for the Greek text has *mina*, which was only one-tenth of a pound. A *mina* of silver was worth about twenty dollars, but it was a substantial amount for it was about three months wages for a working man.)[18] The nobleman goes away to be invested with ruling authority and return. The servants are left among their fellow citizens who oppose the idea of the nobleman ruling over them, so they send representatives to witness against his investment with that authority.

When the nobleman returns, he begins to call for an accounting of the servants' results of trading with his money. One reports a return of ten *minas* for the one *mina*, and in turn in commended and rewarded with management of ten cities. A second reports a return of five *minas* for the one *mina*, and in turn is rewarded with management of five cities. A third servant confesses his fear of the master and his lack of confidence in himself to invest the master's money so he hid it to guard its safety. The nobleman condemns him and takes the one *mina* with no gain and gives it to the servant who has been most effective.

The Matthew parable concludes with the unprofitable servant being cast into "outer darkness," while the Luke parable concludes with harsh punishment of the people who oppose the nobleman.

…

If we are trusted with gifts or talents or resources, we are accountable to use them for their purpose. If we are effective, we will have the good fortune to see the fruits of our labors (investments). But if we do not use the talents or resources we have, they are as worthless as if we never had them. And unused talents, skills, and resources are vulnerable to being lost or wasted.

…

NOTES

[1]Morgan P. Noyes, "1 Timothy, Exposition," *Interpreter's Bible*, vol. 11 (New York: Abingdon, 1955), 414; John B. Noss, *Man's Religions* (New York: MacMillan, 1956), 524; "The Devil in the Bible," *History Magazine*, https://www.history.com/topics/folklore/history-of-the-devil#section_1 (accessed Mar. 20, 2019).

[2]Lewis M. Hopfe and Mark R. Woodward, *Religions of the World* (Upper Saddle River, NJ: Pearson/Prentice-Hall, 2005), 226.

[3]Samuel Prideaux Tregelles, *Gesenius' Hebrew and Chaldee Lexicon of the Old Testament* (Grand Rapids: Eerdmans, 1950), 758; Jay P. Green, trans., *The Interlinear Hebrew-Aramaic Old Testament* (London: Trinitarian Bible Society, 1994), 639 (Jdgs. 3:28).

[4]Eugene H. Peterson, *The Message* (Colorado Springs, CO: NAVPRESS, 2005), 1670.

[5]William F. Arndt and F. Wilbur Gingrich, trans., *Bauer's Greek-English Lexicon of the New Testament* (Chicago: University of Chicago Press, 1979), 345, 656-57; G. Abbott-Smith, *A Manual Greek Lexicon of the New Testament* (Edinburgh: T. & T. Clark, 1950), 199, 360.

[6]*Bauer's Lexicon*, 338ic.

[7]Kate Louise Roberts, comp., *Hoyt's New Cyclopedia of Practical Quotations* (New York: Funk and Wagnalls, 1940), 371 (14).

[8]Abbott-Smith, *Lexicon*, 293; Tregelles, *Genesius' Lexicon*, 792.

[9]Source unknown.

[10]*Bauer's Lexicon*, 138, 849-50 (2).

[11]Ibid., 140.

[12]Ibid., 450a2b.

[13]Abbott-Smith, *Lexicon*, 157; *Bauer's Lexicon*, 269.

[14]Abbott-Smith, *Lexicon*, 421, 455; *Bauer's Lexicon*, 772b3.

[15]Abbott-Smith, *Lexicon*, 106.

[16] *Bauer's Lexicon*, 632b2d.

[17] *mi yodeya*, Jewish website, "Will Moshiach Be Immortal?" https://judaism.stackexchange.com/questions/75895/will-moshiach-be-immortal (accessed Mar. 22, 2019). Note the promise of eternal sovereignty in Mic. 4:7; Ezek. 43:7-9; Dan. 4:34, 12:7; Heb. 1:8, and Rev. 22:5.

[18] Paul Scherer, "The Gospel According to Luke, Exposition," *The Interpreter's Bible*, vol. 8 (New York: Abingdon Press,1952), 330.

Pre-Passion Days in Jerusalem

(Luke 19:28–21:38)

ARRIVAL IN JERUSALEM

(19:28-48)

As Jesus approaches Bethany, just over the crest of the Mount of Olives to the east of Jerusalem, he sends two of his disciples to get a donkey for him to ride into Jerusalem. (Jesus has probably made arrangement in advance with the owner of the donkey.) As Jesus nears the city, riding the donkey, the crowds cry, "Blessed is the king who comes in the name of the Lord."

Then Jesus sees Jerusalem. His love for the city and its great heritage and symbolism, along with his deep disappointment and hurt because of the way Jewish religious leaders have violated its true purpose, causes him to weep and say, "Would that even today you knew the things that make for peace."

The description of the entry into the city has been traditionally believed to be a messianic demonstration, citing the attitude of the crowd. I dare to differ. The crowd certainly wanted to make the situation about Jesus being their hoped-for Messiah. Jesus' choice to ride a donkey, I believe, was "one last message" to the crowd that he had not come to be a "conquering deliverer."

Jesus then enters the Temple, where he rebukes those who have so violated the place dedicated to the worship of God and that has such a noble history. His action in "cleansing the Temple" indicates he has come to the very center of Jewish power to challenge the corruption and arrogance that have developed in the Jewish hierarchy of the priesthood.

The priests and Levites who control the Temple, who are responsible for its operations and maintenance, also receive their livelihood from portions of the animals and agricultural products brought for sacrifice, as had been set forth by Moses in the regulations about sacrifices and by Joshua in the division of the land to the tribes (see Leviticus 7 and Joshua 21). They obviously keep flocks of approved sacrificial animals for sale as a service to pilgrims who travel from distances and need to secure them locally. The Temple tax is a specified Jewish coin (Exod. 30:11-16), so pilgrims need to exchange their Roman money for the approved coins.

> What began as a service for the benefit of pilgrims has become a business for the priests and Levites. Business competition causes the different shepherds, salesmen of doves, and coin exchangers to press closer and closer to the temple until the Temple itself has become what Jesus calls "a den of robbers." Obviously, the tradesmen have developed seedy reputations by some of their practices. The place needs a good "cleaning out."

Whereas Mark records that at the end of the day Jesus and his disciples leave the city, probably returning to Bethany or the Mount of Olives, Luke simply states that Jesus continues teaching daily in the temple. The Jewish leaders now are even more determined to "destroy" him, but they have to deal with his popularity among the people. Strategy becomes their primary concern.

For the religious leaders it is no longer a question of whether or not they can "pull it off," but of how and when. Their positions of power, prestige, and influence have been challenged and threatened. This they will not tolerate from a "peasant preacher" whom they consider to be a blasphemer.

PASSION WEEK DEVELOPS
(20:1-8)

During the first days of Holy Week, Jesus continues to come into Jerusalem to teach and preach in the temple and then leaves the city at night. The people in authority challenge him as they believe they have every right to do.

The tribe of Levi, including Aaron and his descendants who were the hereditary priesthood, had been assigned by Moses to do the required sacrifices, care for the Tabernacle/Temple, and receive portions of all those sacrifices as their inheritance instead of having a portion of the land allotted to them. If Jesus is not a Levite, he has no right to teach there. (The genealogies in both Matthew and Luke indicate that Mary and Joseph were of the tribe of Judah, not Levi.) It seems the questioners are not really concerned about the tribal heritage of Jesus, but this just gives them another thing they can trouble him about as they try to discredit him.

Jesus responds to the authorities' question with a question, something he is recorded to have done often. He asks their judgment about John's baptism. His questioners recognize that he has given them a dilemma for which they have no acceptable answer. The answer they would like to give they dare not give. While they are happy to have the positions of religious authority, they have to answer, "We do not know." Jesus refuses to respond to them any further. There is an implication behind this story, as if Jesus has asked the elders, "If you don't understand basic things such as the nature of baptism, how can you consider yourselves reliable leaders of religion for others?" (It reminds us of the question Jesus asks Nicodemus in John 3:10, "Are you a teacher of Israel, and yet you do not understand this?")

ISRAEL'S UNFAITHFULNESS
(20:9-18)

Jesus tells a parable about a vineyard and tenants that describe how the leaders of the Israelite people have failed them. The owner of the vineyard entrusts his land to tenants to care for in his absence. Instead of managing the vineyard for the interest of the owner, they care only for themselves and ill-treat those who come for the fruits from the vineyard. This happens twice and then the owner sends his son, expecting that surely he will be respected. The tenants instead choose to kill the heir and seize the vineyard for themselves.

The crowd hearing the parable cries, "God forbid." They seem to be saying, "That surely couldn't happen here!" But Jesus replies, "That is exactly what has happened here." The people who were supposed to build the nation have instead rejected the very cornerstone on which the whole structure would rest. Without a foundation, a building cannot stand, and in falling will crush those in its path.

This parable uncovers a vital and fundamental difference between Old Testament religion and New Testament religion. The records in the Old Testament reflect that for the most part the people thought the purpose of religion was to obey commandments about sacrifices, rituals, and prohibitions in order to please God and receive favorable treatment by him. There were voices that called on them to be just in conduct and upright in their lives, but the masses did not get the point that becoming in character like God was the true purpose of religion. Like the tenants in the vineyard, the leaders who shaped the meaning of Jewish religion did not "produce that fruit" for God through the centuries.

Jesus, the son in the parable, has come to change that. The central focus of his preaching is, "Repent and believe the gospel." Repentance and faith, if they are authentic, result in a complete transformation in a person's life—a new life in harmony with God. This is the "fruit" of religion that God designed, the purpose of religion that the Son became incarnate to reveal, the foundation stone upon which true believers are built into the kingdom of God, and the foundation of our eternal hope. Name it this way: the purpose of religion is to transform trusting people into the character of God so we can be redeemed from alienation by forgiveness and brought into reconciled harmony with God, belonging again in the Eden of God's paradise from which sinfulness has shut us out. Any other meaning, purpose, and practice of religion is a faulty foundation that will cause the structures of religious institutions to fall in failure around us.

OUTWITTING HIS ADVERSARIES
(20:19-38)

The Jewish religious leaders and Jesus are in open opposition. As long as Jesus was in Galilee his teachings and actions were just a thorn in the flesh to them. Now he has come to Jerusalem and is openly teaching in the temple area, confronting them in their own place of authority. He is a real threat to their positions with the Romans and is influencing the people by teaching what the Jewish leaders consider blasphemy. They recognize the previous parable about treacherous servants as being about them. Their determination to destroy Jesus deepens.

The Jewish leaders intend to get him in trouble both politically and religiously. They ask about paying tribute to Caesar. If Jesus says, "No," he is in trouble with the Romans. If he says, "Yes," he faces trouble with the Jews who hate their subjection to the Romans. Jesus turns the authorities' question back on them: "Look at the money and tell me whose image is on it." They have to admit that it is Roman money with Caesar's image on it. Jesus then presents them with an answer that foils their design. One more devious test by them is thwarted, but another will come.

This time it is Sadducees who believe they can use one of their theological beliefs to trap Jesus and discredit him with a larger group of the people. (The Sadducees do not believe in resurrection because it is not set forth in the Pentateuch, but the Pharisees are deeply committed to the hope [see Acts 23:8].)

The questioners cite a long-held Jewish practice of a brother marrying a brother's widow to raise children for a deceased childless brother. (This practice developed out of the ancient Hebrew belief that after death, people live on in their children instead of having a future life after resurrection.) The Sadducees set up a crafty situation: Seven brothers all marry the same wife, but none birth children. Their trick question: "Now in this resurrection—which we don't believe in to begin with—whose wife is this woman going to be?"

Jesus replies with a truth about the difference between life in the physical world and life in the spiritual world. He describes marriage as belonging to life in the physical world, involving exclusive covenant, physical intimacy, and reproduction, as it is being practiced among them. In the world of spirit beyond physical life these features of physical life and reproduction will not be features of life in the spiritual realm. And Jesus refutes their denial of resurrection by describing God as the God of the living and not of the dead. Without saying so, Jesus also frees those who hear him from the dread and fear of *Hades*, the place of the dead, to which Hebrews have long believed to be their fate at death, a place where the dead go to gradually fade away into a shadowy existence. His opponents have been routed again.

UNTRUSTWORTHY LEADERS
(20:39-47)

The remainder of Luke 20 records an ongoing conversation with some scribes or rabbis, authorities in the provisions and requirements of the Mosaic law. (These teachers came into prominence after the Babylonian Exile when much of the Hebrew Scriptures had been put into written form and the synagogue had become an important center for teaching the Torah. They were the copiers of the scrolls and the recognized authorities about their content and meaning.)

In this passage the scribes acknowledge that Jesus has put them to shame so they dare not ask him any more questions. So Jesus puts them to the test. He asks them to explain the relationship of David to the Messiah: Do the scriptures teach that the Messiah will be David's Son or David's Lord? No answer from them is recorded.

Jesus concludes by warning the people to beware of religious leaders who are more interested in recognitions and honors than they are in human needs and service, whose own religion cannot measure up to the standard of authenticity.

TRUE GENEROSITY
(21:1-4)

In the temple Jesus sees actions that give him an opportunity to teach a lesson about giving. A widow gives all she has, though just a pittance. The rich give much more impressive amounts that most likely make no dent in their wealth or lifestyle. In terms of the temple's treasury the difference is significant, but the evaluation Jesus makes is about the meaning of the gift. He says the widow gives more than all of them. Maybe that means the significance of a gift is not determined by what we give but by what we have left. Stewardship has to do with the degree of our devotion to the cause for which we give.

PREPARING FOR APOCALYPTIC TIMES
(21:5-28)

Luke's passage about "end times" is parallel to Matthew 24 and Mark 13. Apparently the heightened activity of the Passover festival and the presence of Jesus and his followers in Jerusalem have caused intense interest in the messianic hope, along with growing anticipation that maybe Jesus is really the Messiah. Someone, perhaps a disciple, calls attention to the magnificence of the temple. Jesus replies that it will be destroyed. In turn his followers ask when this will happen and how they can know it is at hand. Jesus answers that warnings of disaster will come and conflicts will happen, but these will not be signs of the end.

Jesus then tells them what they can expect in the ongoing events of their lives and of history. National conflicts and natural disasters will be a part of the world's situations. Those who follow Jesus can expect to have opposition, but this will be an opportunity for them to bear testimony to their faith and they can be sure of God's help to answer. Jesus encourages them to be faithful even though they can expect times of distress and suffering, for the city of Jerusalem will be devastated. He warns them to escape the violence if they can. He concludes with a word of hope: when earthly trials come to an end, redemption will bring deliverance.

AN EARTHLY MESSIANIC KINGDOM
(21:29-38)

Following the discourse about "end times" traditions, Luke records some guiding counsel by Jesus for his followers. In a parable Jesus explains that what can be expected in human affairs is as certain as the changing of the seasons. You understand readily that the budding of a fig tree and the beginning of summer always come together, he tells them. The lesson seems to be that when pride and greed, egotism and competition, hate and vengeance play out in human affairs, it is equally certain that conflicts and wars will happen.

Jesus assures his followers that it will all happen in their own generation, and that he will give them words of counsel that will not pass away. He encourages them not to lose heart in the turmoil of life's experiences but to practice prayer, to avoid dissipate living, and to be watchful and always ready to stand "before the Son of man."

Luke adds a summary statement about Jesus spending his days in the temple and his nights on the Mount of Olives, and that the people come daily to hear him teach.

Conspiracy, Condemnation, and Crucifixion

(Luke 22:1–23:56)

THE CLIMAX OF CONTROVERSY

(22:1-6)

The Passover and an eight-day Feast of Unleavened Bread to follow will start the next Sabbath. The Passover meal will be eaten after sundown on Friday, as soon as the Sabbath begins, so all preparations must be made on Friday before sundown.

Jerusalem is crowded with throngs of pilgrims. Jesus had come into the city in a prominent procession on the previous Sunday and stirred up things by his challenge to the "powerful" in the temple. Messianic hope is high among many of the people. The Roman authorities are being especially watchful for any budding disturbance. The Jewish religious leaders have a dilemma on their hands. They want Jesus dead and no longer a trouble to them, but they have found no way to get him killed without raising a storm of reaction among the crowds who are following him and hanging onto his teachings.

On Monday and Tuesday, Jesus comes into the city and the temple and addresses the crowds openly. Then on Wednesday night or Thursday morning one of the disciples, Judas Iscariot, approaches the Jewish leaders and offers to betray Jesus by helping them find an occasion to arrest him away from the crowds. The Scriptures do not reveal Judas' motivation for his betrayal, but the leaders promise him a reward for his help.

THURSDAY EVENING SUPPER

(22:7-13)

On Jesus' instructions Peter and John go and prepare for their evening meal in a guest upper room. Jesus has likely made an earlier agreement with the owner of the house to have the room available. Although Luke refers to the day when all leaven must be removed from homes before the Feast of Unleavened Bread and the day Passover lambs will be sacrificed—two events that happen on Friday—the events recorded here surely occur on Thursday, and the meal is a preparatory meal, a seder, and not the Passover meal itself.

UNDERSTANDING THE UNCERTAIN

(22:14-23)

The Synoptic Gospels are quite alike in their records of the Last Supper. There are variations in, and some interpreters believe additions to, the record of what Jesus says and means as he and the apostles share the bread and cup that become the elements of the Lord's Supper (the Eucharist).

According to Luke, Jesus makes a statement about not drinking "of the fruit of the vine until the kingdom of God comes," a reference to the widely held belief in Jewish apocalyptic traditions that the beginning of the messianic kingdom would be celebrated with a great feast. Jesus then blesses the elements of the supper and shares them with his disciples.

Only Luke records that Jesus says, "Do this in remembrance of me." Some language specialists say that in Aramaic (the language Jesus almost surely used) the verb "to be" would not be spoken. The translated phrase should thus be, "This means my body" instead of "This is my body," indicating representation rather than identification.

John does not include a record about the bread and cup, but does tell of Jesus washing the disciples' feet and the things he says to them after the supper and before they go to Gethsemane.

All four Gospels record that Jesus exposes Judas as the traitor who will betray him. Matthew and Mark record the exposure while they are eating but before the bread and cup. Luke records the exposure after the bread and cup. John records the exposure after the finish of the meal and the washing of the disciples' feet. If Luke and John are correct about the sequence of events, then Judas is present and shares the bread and cup and has his feet washed by Jesus before he goes out into the night to do his dastardly deed of treachery.

· · ·

The events of Holy Week were chaotic and traumatic for the disciples, and they still could not comprehend the meaning of a crucified Messiah. A lack of understanding continued during the years following the death and resurrection of Jesus. The early Christians faced great changes and had no established authority to guide them.

As followers of Jesus, their faith and practices were so different from the prevailing doctrines and rituals of Judaism that the Christians were both persecuted and driven out of the synagogues. The old rituals of Judaism didn't fit their new faith as followers of Jesus. They had to make choices and decisions as they found their way into what became first-century Christianity. They developed the traditions that two generations later were recorded as the first writing of the documents that are the four Gospels. I do not find it surprising, nor troubling, that memories about events such as the relation of the Last Supper to the Jewish Passover were not all the same.

· · ·

SUCH HUMAN DISCIPLES
(22:24-30)

Only Luke records the dispute among the disciples about who should be regarded as the greatest, although it is the subject of discussion at other times. There appear to be behind these concerns a reflection of aspirations about places of recognition and prominence in the hoped-for messianic kingdom.

As in other places where this discussion of rank and privilege is recorded, Jesus is clear in his words to the disciples: That kind of ranking belongs to life in this earthly world, where whoever gets to sit at the table and be served is considered a person of prominence and authority. But this is not the value system that belongs to the kingdom of God and those in it. In verses 29-30, however, Jesus makes promises that seem to reverse what he has just said about greatness.

...

I find comparable statements of "kingdom privilege" only in eschatological passages referring to messianic promises. I also believe that the history of the Christian church indicates that the same "human" interest in recognition and priority ranking has been of great concern to many in the structures of religious organizational leadership. It is deceptively easy to talk about "humble ministry" while at the same time pursuing "princely privilege." The Eternal God, who has infinite inherent greatness, has revealed himself as the greatest unselfish giver seeking to serve the greatest need of us all through his caring love, compassionate forgiveness, and reconciling grace. That's true greatness.

...

PREPARATION FOR THE INCOMPREHENSIBLE
(22:31-38)

The theme turns to warning. With insight, either divine or truly perceptive, Jesus knows that the determined opposition of the Jewish religious leaders is surely about to secure his death. Arrogant power will destroy any challenge, if possible. Jesus knows also that this will cause great trauma, confusion, and fear among the disciples. He addresses Simon Peter, though he intends the warning for all of them.

In verse 31 Jesus uses the plural pronoun "you," but in verse 32 the pronoun "you" is singular, appearing to indicate that Jesus is challenging Peter to be a "rock" for his fellow disciples through the trials ahead.

Peter, in his typical way, boasts that he can really be counted on. Jesus warns him that he is boasting about more than he knows, more than he will be able to fulfill, and so will deny Jesus that very night. The disciples cannot comprehend what lies ahead for them.

Jesus then questions them about instructions he had given them earlier when he sent them on missions. They agree that they have been provided for. Now Jesus instructs them to prepare for the turmoil and peril that lie ahead.

Jesus' instruction to the disciples to buy swords is problematic, seemingly contradicting his later refusal to let Peter use the sword in Gethsemane (vv. 49-51), and also his words to Pilate, ". . . if my kingdom were of this world, my servants would fight, that I might not be handed over to the Jews" (John 18:36).

IN THE GARDEN
(22:39-46)

The Gethsemane story is shorter in Luke than in Matthew and Mark. Luke records two parts of the event: Jesus' admonition to the disciples to pray for sustaining help and his own prayer for the will of the Father to be done. Some ancient manuscripts of Luke add the image of "sweat like drops of blood" to describe the soul struggle of Jesus. None of the other Gospels include this.

The manuscripts considered most reliable do not include references of "sweat like drops of blood," and the often-stated description that Jesus "sweated blood" is not supported by this text. The word translated "like" is a compound word that is conditional and descriptive (*os* = as, *ei* = if, *osei* = as if), describing sweat "as if" blood, not calling it drops of blood. This comment in the Lukan tradition seems surely to have been a scribal addition.

The reference to the sleeping disciples describes them as no doubt exhausted by the hectic activity of the previous days. And despite the warnings Jesus has given them, they have not grasped the reality of his imminent death.

BETRAYAL AND ARREST
(22:47-54)

Judas and his collaborators come upon the scene in Gethsemane. Luke calls them a crowd. Matthew and Mark describe them as representatives of the Jewish leaders (chief priests and elders). John writes that a band of soldiers and their officers accompany Jesus. These are all Jewish, however, for the Romans do not come into the picture until after the Jewish trials.

All three of the Synoptic Gospels record that Judas betrays Jesus to the officers with a kiss, as he has agreed with the authorities to do. John records that Jesus identifies himself to the officers and asks that the disciples not be arrested.

The impetuous Peter draws his sword and strikes one of the men. Characteristic of Jesus, he tells Peter to stop—in contrast to his uncharacteristic earlier advice to the disciples to buy swords (v. 36).

The officers arrest Jesus, as they have been brought along to do, and take him to the high priest's house, where they keep him prisoner until about dawn.

UNPREPARED DISCIPLES
(22:55-62)

Peter follows, at a distance, and mingles with the crowd in the outside courtyard. Three times he is accosted and accused. Three times he denies any association with Jesus. The disciples prove by their actions of desertion that they are not able to live up to their claims of loyalty and courage made earlier to Jesus. Peter and John (according to the Fourth Gospel) show the most courage until Peter is accused and, after the cock crows, goes away and weeps in contrition. Nothing more is said about John until he is near the cross with Mary.

THE JEWISH TRIALS
(22:63-71)

Luke includes a shorter record of the Jewish trials than Matthew and Mark, and he describes them as taking place after dawn. The night guards abuse Jesus with mockery and violence until they take him before the council (Sanhedrin). The Jewish trials are about blasphemy. The council questions Jesus about whether he claims to be the Messiah and Son of God. Jesus answers them by pointing out that they are accusing him of claiming the very things they have been saying about him. Their verdict is what they have already decided, so they are ready to condemn him. But there is that troublesome issue about having to get the Roman authorities to carry out their evil plan to kill Jesus. They must go to Pilate.

TROUBLESOME ROMANS
(23:1-7)

The Jewish leaders have a new problem on their hands. They know that the Roman governor will not care about their religious quarrels over claims of messiahship or deity, as long as they do not cause him trouble from Rome. So far as Pilate is concerned, their quarrel is about "petty religion," but his relationship with Rome is about influential power.

Before Pilate, the Jews make a political charge against Jesus: treason and insurrection, activities they know Pilate will dare not ignore. They accuse Jesus of claiming to be a king, not a Jewish deity—a shrewd political manipulation. After questioning Jesus, Pilate is convinced that Jesus presents no problem for him and tells the Jewish crowd so. They roar their disapproval, and Pilate hears a reference to Galilee. He thinks he sees a way out, so he sends Jesus to Herod Antipas.

FAILURE OF AN EVASIVE SCHEME

(23:8-16)

Although Herod has charge of Galilee, he is in Jerusalem, apparently for the Passover festival. He seems to like the attention he is getting from the Roman governor by this referral. He also wants to satisfy his own curiosity about Jesus—perhaps he may get to see one of Jesus' "miracles."

Jesus refuses to honor these "kangaroo court" tactics by responding to questions. Herod joins the Jewish leaders and the soldiers in mocking and mistreating Jesus. Herod and Pilate put away their previous enmity and become friends after this, even though Herod has done nothing to help Pilate solve his problem. Pilate has the dilemma of deciding how to issue a verdict on one he knows to be innocent, a verdict the scheming Jewish leaders will accept. After all, he will have to keep on dealing with the Jews.

To the raging crowd, Pilate reports that he finds no fault in Jesus on the charges they have made against him, so the only reasonable thing for him to do is have Jesus chastised and released.

A CROWD TURNED MOB

(23:17-25)

The crowd pleads for the release of Barabbas and the crucifixion of Jesus, an incredible choice. Pilate protests that such is not fitting for him to do, but the crowd becomes more and more insistent in their demands. At this point the Jewish leaders change tactics. According to John 19:4-16 the Jewish leaders, realizing that persuasion will not gain their wishes, turn to intimidation. They threaten Pilate that, if he does not have Jesus killed, they will report him to Caesar for letting someone go on pretending to be a rival king. This, of course, will not be tolerated, so Pilate bends to their demand and condemns Jesus to death.

SADISM ON DISPLAY

(23:26-31)

After he is condemned Jesus is mocked, abused, and brutally beaten before he is taken out to be executed. The Fourth Gospel records that Jesus begins the procession to Golgotha bearing his own cross. The Synoptic Gospels record only that Simon is forced to carry the cross. It is thus believed that Jesus begins the procession but falls under the weight of the cross due to weakness from savage abuse since the seizure in Gethsemane. Simon is then forced into service so the execution can be completed, or at least sped up.

Luke alone records the story of the women lamenting the tragic fate Jesus is suffering. Jesus answers their lamentations with a warning that harsh troubles lie ahead for the city.

The proverb about "green wood" and "dry wood" describes the contrast between the consequences of following truth and uprightness on one hand and deceit and folly on the other.

"Green wood" describes a tree in which there is life, and refers to what is being done to Jesus in whom there is the truest of life. "Dry wood" describes a dead tree. ("What shall be done" KJV, or "What will happen" RSV, "when the wood is dry" translates *ti* [what] *genatai* [will come into being, will happen, will be the outcome of].) This figure refers to the "time and eternity" disaster for whoever chooses to live by values that lead to alienation from God and total absence of "abundant life" (see Jas. 1:14-15). An obvious implication is the contrast between the outcome of following one such as Jesus or following the Jewish religious leaders who are securing his execution.

It seems unlikely that Jesus would have been able or allowed to have this kind of conversation with onlookers. At this point he is near total exhaustion. The cruelty of the soldiers and the chaos of the situation most likely would not have permitted it. But the warning attributed to Jesus, and the outcome reflected in the proverb about "green" or "dry" wood are surely accurate about the outcome of the ongoing injustice and the history that follow.

THREE CROSSES
(23:32-33)

The reference to the two other persons also being crucified indicates that, to the Roman soldiers detailed for the execution, the death of Jesus and the two criminals is no more than their day's assignment. The location of the Crucifixion also indicates it is a common execution site. The Fourth Gospel records that the place of execution is near the city, indicating it is outside the city—which would be a concession to Jewish sensitivities about the sacred significance of the city. And, according to Roman practice, posting crosses alongside main highways would strike fear into the hearts of people to help maintain order.

FORGIVENESS VS. INHUMANITY
(23:34-38)

Jesus' statement of forgiveness is not present in some ancient manuscripts, but we can be grateful for those who were inspired to include it. It is so characteristic of the spirit of Jesus, and it stands in radical contrast to the harsh attitudes and actions of the soldiers and some of the crowd gathered around the cross. This is divine love in gracious expression.

As Jesus hangs in agony, voicing forgiveness for those around him, soldiers crassly gamble for his clothing. Those who manipulated his death scoff at him now with mocking about messianic images that many common people have come to believe. They taunt him with challenge to use his "miracle working power" for himself as he "supposedly" has done for others. The soldiers join in the mocking by challenging him to prove he can free himself from their execution and by offering him vinegar—probably drugged—as though they care about the agony of his fate.

Following their practice of placing a sign on the cross stating the crime of a condemned person, the Romans place an inscription on Jesus' cross referring to him as "King of the Jews." John's Gospel notes that the priests dicker with Pilate about the wording of the sign: They want it to state that this is a claim by Jesus and not something they accept as valid. Pilate holds his ground, however. The wording of the sign may indicate that Pilate regards Jesus in higher esteem than he does the Jewish leaders who by plotting and intimidation had Jesus crucified. The proclamation stands for all time as an awesome word of truth.

UNFOUNDED PLEADING AND HUMBLE PENITENCE
(23:39-43)

The criminals hanging on either side of Jesus react to him in radically different ways. One of them seems almost to join the mocking crowd with his plea, "save yourself and us." The other shows evidence of penitence and confession in his plea for mercy. On the procession to Golgotha, during the activities of the Crucifixion, and hearing the words of Jesus from the cross, the criminal evidently recognizes something about Jesus that makes him believe Jesus will indeed overcome in the end. Jesus promises him a presence in paradise.

The prevailing belief in Judaism was that at death a person went into *sheol* (the place of the dead) where both good and bad went. Pharisees who came to believe in resurrection believed that souls waited in *sheol* until resurrection and judgment. Sadducees who did not believe in resurrection would have held to the belief that at death the soul went to sheol and there faded away to a shadowy existence. The concept of paradise was adopted from Persian beliefs about a "walled garden" of existence in a state of blessed peacefulness.

The promise by Jesus to the penitent criminal gives a new facet to the varied beliefs about existence after death. Instead of temporary existence awaiting an end-time resurrection and judgment, Jesus promised the dying man that he would be with him in paradise on that day. It seems that Jesus gave an entirely new orientation to the experience of physical death and the state of existence for people after physical death. This understanding about existence after death is in harmony with the passage in John 11:23-26, where Martha says of Lazarus, "I know he will rise again in the resurrection at the last day." Jesus then spoke in the present, "I am the resurrection and the life."

A personal relationship with Jesus will surely not be voided by physical death. We cannot comprehend the details while still mortal, but the certainty we can surely trust. What awesome "surprises" await us in eternity!

THE DEATH OF JESUS

(23:44-49)

There are minor differences in the Gospel records about times on the day of the Crucifixion. This may be the result of differences in the way Jews and Romans counted time, or it may be the result of variances that developed in the traditions that came down to the Gospel writers through the nearly two generations before the Gospels were written. There is agreement, however, about most of the sequence of events.

1. Jesus is judged by Jews and Romans in the early hours of Friday morning.
2. The Crucifixion takes place about midmorning.
3. From about noon till midafternoon there is an unnatural darkness.
4. About midafternoon Jesus dies. (According to John, this was earlier than expected by the soldiers, for it was not unusual for crucified people to linger much longer before dying.)

The recorded incidents of unexpected darkness and earthquake evidently strike fear into the soldiers and the crowd. Matthew and Mark both record that the centurion in command remarks that surely Jesus is "the Son of God." Luke writes that the centurion says, "Certainly this man was innocent," and the crowd goes away "beating their breasts."

Mark writes that when Jesus is arrested his disciples forsake him and flee. Luke records that at the Crucifixion a group of his followers "stood at a distance and saw all these things." John writes that a small group, including Mary, stays close enough to the cross for Jesus to talk to Mary and John.

The Synoptic Gospels all record that the curtain of the temple is torn open, possibly by the earthquake. According to tradition, this is the curtain that closed off the Holy of Holies except to the high priest on the Day of Atonement. The tearing of the curtain came to symbolize that the presence of God is now open to all people.

A HASTY BURIAL

(23:50-56)

After it is established that Jesus is dead—and with permission from Pilate—Joseph (assisted by Nicodemus, according to John) takes the body from the cross, performs temporary preparation for burial, and places the body in a nearby tomb. The shortness of time and the approach of the Sabbath make the temporary burial necessary. It is midafternoon and the Jewish Sabbath will begin at sundown. Jewish custom requires that dead bodies not be left hanging on crosses during the Sabbath.

Some devoted women prepare the appropriate materials for a proper permanent burial after the Sabbath. Then they rest on the Sabbath. It surely is a sad and seemingly hopeless feeling.

Resurrection, Recovery, and Conclusion

(Luke 24:1-33)

DIVINE VICTORY VS. HUMAN EVIL
(24:1-12)

The women who prepared Jesus' body for burial on Friday find his tomb empty on Sunday morning shortly after dawn. Several followers of Jesus experience his resurrected presence with them. The circumstances of the appearances vary, but there are some common features. The "living" Jesus has a bodily form that is sometimes recognizable but at other times not until he does or says something that makes him known. His bodily form is not subject to natural laws of matter, for he appears without the normal limitations of walls or patterns of physical movement.

The Easter stories begin in each Gospel with the followers of Jesus expecting nothing but that he is dead. Mark and Luke record that the women who first visit the tomb have gone there to complete the proper preparation of the body that had been buried so hastily on Friday. There are variances in the traditions about who goes first, but all agree there is a "messenger" (or messengers) who informs the women that Jesus is alive.

- Matthew 28:2, 5 describes the messenger as *aggelos* (translated "angel," but the basic meaning of the Greek word is "messenger" or "one who carries a message"). The "angel" identification comes from other descriptive words such as "white raiment," "white robe," "dazzling apparel," and "in white."
- Mark 16:5 records ". . . they saw a young man."
- Luke 24:4 reads "two men stood by them," but the disciples at Emmaus call them *aggelon* (24:23).
- John records an appearance to Mary Magdalene by two *aggelous* (20:12) and by Jesus (20:14-16).

When the followers who have gone to the tomb report to the others that the tomb is empty, those who have not seen the empty tomb find it hard to believe. Not surprisingly, an unbelievably momentous event has occurred.

...

The familiar stories of "resurrection morning" are a source of great assurance and inspiration, but the event itself is also full of awe, mystery, and even questions. We who live in a realm of physical experience—a world of time, space, and matter—cannot imagine what it is like to exist in the realm of spirit where matter is no longer a factor. "The veil of death" leaves us with questions for which we have no answers and mysteries we cannot solve. Faith provides the foundation on which we need to anchor our attempt to understand the meaning of Jesus' resurrection.

The nature of resurrection is beyond human comprehension. We know from physical experience and scientific examination what happens to a physical body when it dies. Life is not an entity that animates a body, can leave the body, and return to the body to animate it again. Therefore, resurrection is a mystery we cannot understand.

Some facts underlying our faith as Christians are important as we try to understand what resurrection means for us. I believe the words of Jesus that "God is spirit" (John 4:24) are absolute truth. Nothing else will fit in our faith that God is the source and creator of all that exists in the physical universe. For creation of material to be true, then a spirit/person must exist before and be the designer/source for the existence of the material. This cannot be proved in laboratory tests, but nothing else can account for the marvel and order of the physical universe and human life.

We believe that the Eternal Son shared a fullness of spiritual entity (divine Spirit) before the Incarnation when he "took the form of a servant and was born in the likeness of men" (Phil. 2:7). The Son of God did not need a physical body to be fully real. He became a human person with a body because we needed his human presence among us so we could grasp the revelation of God's character and reconciling purpose for which he came into the world (2 Cor. 5:19).

After the Crucifixion Jesus did not need a physical body to be as fully the Eternal Son as he was before the Incarnation. The disciples needed the appearances after the Resurrection to enable them to believe that the Eternal Son was victorious over physical death, that spirit transcends matter, and that the true person—both human and divine—is the spirit/soul. The living Christ appeared to the disciples for their benefit, not his. The assurance of his victory over physical death became the foundational basis for Christian hope.

...

APPEARANCES TO THE DISCIPLES

(24:13-49)

After the morning events at the empty tomb, Jesus appears to two disciples on the road to Emmaus. No reason is recorded for their journey, but as would be expected they are talking about the "things that had happened." Then Jesus appears and walks and talks with them, but they do not recognize him until he agrees to "stay" with them and break bread. Then Jesus vanishes. Though it is late in the day, the disciples hurry back to Jerusalem to share their experience with the others.

Jesus later appears among the gathered disciples (minus Judas and Thomas). They are startled by his presence, so he speaks words of assurance to calm their anxiety. Luke alone records that Jesus eats a piece of broiled fish to assure them he is real and not a ghostly apparition. (We have to wonder if this was a later addition to the tradition to strengthen its credibility.)

Jesus talks with the disciples and helps them remember the hopes held and expressed in their ancient religious traditions, leading them to better understand the meaning of his death. Looking forward, he helps them grasp the purpose of God that forgiveness and repentance are to be proclaimed as good news to all people. He reminds them that they have witnessed what God has done, and then assigns them—with the promised presence and aid of the Holy Spirit (v. 49)—to be witnesses about it to others. Jesus instructs them to remain in Jerusalem until that presence and power becomes a reality in their lives.

INCARNATION COMPLETED
(24:50-53)

Luke ends his gospel with a brief account of the ascension of Jesus, then he opens the book of Acts with a fuller record about the ascension and the commission by Jesus to his followers. The conclusion of Luke's Gospel and the introduction to Acts also record the faithful obedience and the bold response by the disciples as brave practitioners and proclaimers of their faith in Jerusalem while they wait for Pentecost. The origin of the Christian religion and the Christian church come to life in the nucleus of pilgrims who trust Jesus in life and through his death. We are eternally in their debt.

CPSIA information can be obtained
at www.ICGtesting.com
Printed in the USA
LVHW081417120519
617531LV00040B/2349/P